Ronald Fletcher was Professor of Sociology at the University of York until he decided to take up full-time writing and broadcasting. His previous publications include *The Biography of a Victorian Village* and *The Parkers at Saltram, 1769–1798* which formed the basis of a BBC 2 series, in addition to many works of sociology. Much of his recent work in social history has been based on the East Anglian area where he now lives. As this book goes to press he is making a partial return to academic life, now holding a part-time professorship at the University of Reading.

Ronald Fletcher

In a Country Churchyard

PALADIN
GRANADA PUBLISHING
London Toronto Sydney New York

Published by Granada Publishing Limited
in Paladin Books 1980

ISBN 0 586 08342 1

First published in Great Britain by
B.T. Batsford Ltd 1978
Copyright © Ronald Fletcher 1978

Granada Publishing Limited
Frogmore, St Albans, Herts AL2 2NF
and
3 Upper James Street, London W1R 4BP
866 United Nations Plaza, New York, NY 10017, USA
117 York Street, Sydney, NSW 2000, Australia
100 Skyway Avenue, Rexdale, Ontario, M9W 3A6, Canada
PO Box 84165, Greenside, 2034 Johannesburg, South Africa
CML Centre, Queen & Wyndham, Auckland 1, New Zealand

Filmset in 'Monophoto' Ehrhardt 10 on 12 pt and
printed in Great Britain by
Fletcher & Son Ltd, Norwich

Granada ®
Granada Publishing ®

Contents

Rejoice, ye dead, where'er your spirits dwell,
Rejoice that yet on earth your fame is bright,
And that your names, remembered day and night,
Live on the lips of those who loved you well.

Preface

The introduction which follows describes the conception and nature of this book, but I would like to mention one significant point separately here: this is also a book of a television series – but not in any ordinary way. A television series was not, in this case, turned into a book, nor the book into a television series. The two were conceived together, resting on a very strong persuasion I have come to have that television can make a positive and distinctive contribution to social history.

These stories – long hidden in East Anglian country churchyards – about the people who made our communities what they are, and who therefore lie at the roots of much of our own nature, are often about 'ordinary' people not known to the orthodox historical record of books and documents. Facts can be reliably discovered about them – from photographs, newspaper accounts, letters, even magic lantern slides – to form a book like this, but television can do something more. The places and situations where these people lived, where the significant stories of their lives took place, are still there, and have barely changed. Television can therefore do what nothing else can do in providing a faithful dramatic reconstruction. People and their stories can, almost literally, be brought to life again. This book, then, is part of an effort to bring together the established methods of social history and the possibilities of television to provide a richer reconstruction of the past than would otherwise be possible.

Social history itself is still very new, but in the complexities of our large-scale society – which often obscure the world and any sense of personal significance from us – it seems to me that, in these ways, it can add many important dimensions of humanity to our knowledge of the past, and so help us towards a fuller understanding of both past and present, and – perhaps? – towards more satisfying perspectives for living.

Grateful acknowledgements are due to John Johnston, Douglas Salmon and Christopher Lewis of BBC Norwich – and to Aubrey Singer, Controller of BBC 2, for the encouragement and assistance he gave to myself and to the region – who made the television side of this possible; to all the staff of the Suffolk County Archive Department at Ipswich; to the *East Anglian Daily Times* who have made available many illustrations; and to all those – far too numerous, alas, to mention individually – who helped in uncovering the material of the several stories.

RONALD FLETCHER
Southwold, September 1977

The author and publishers would like to thank the following for permission to reproduce illustrations: the *East Anglian Daily Times* (page 51 (both)); Oxford University Press (page 93); the *Radio Times* (pages 74 & 77) and the Radio Times Hulton Picture Library (page 47 (top)). The photographs on pages 38 & 48 are Crown Copyright, reproduced by permission of the National Monuments Record.

Introduction

> The curfew tolls the knell of parting day,
>   The lowing herd winds slowly o'er the lea,
> The ploughman homeward plods his weary way,
>   And leaves the world to darkness and to me ...

'Elegy Written in a Country Church-yard'

Gray's elegy, as it is universally known, has always been one of the best-loved English poems, and for good reason. Its quiet, contemplative character, its compassion and wisdom, are faithful to the truth of its subject, and its subject is one we all know. English country churchyards *are* elegies, and the frail memorials they contain commemorate the generations and communities of the past from which you and I have come. Here, if anywhere, lie our foundations.

We always think of graveyards as places of the dead, but recently it has struck me more and more forcibly that they have always been important centres of human *life*. A human community is nothing, it cannot exist, without established traditions, a history, a strong continuity of beliefs, character and values. Like an individual person, a human community is woven out of memory. Everywhere in the world – from the large-scale civilizations of ancient Egypt, Babylon, China, the Indus Valley, with their pyramids, mortuaries and temples, to the smaller intimate communities of the city states of Greece and Rome, and to our own English villages – the places where the ashes of the dead are laid have been the sacred centres of living societies.

Death, and the mystery of it, lie very close to the heart of religion and of our deepest values. The veneration of ancestry is perhaps the strongest cord of human continuity. Remembering the people of the past, their qualities and achievements, their frailties and mistakes, lies close to the heart of culture. And this social truth is one which enters, essentially, into personal sentiment. Some years ago, when my own father was buried,

I realized that this one spot, ordinary though it was – near a gasometer, a coal-pit, a clanking railway siding in the north country – would always be different from any other in the world.

The truth is that wherever men live, work, and make their homes – whether by fishing along the coast, farming in the country, mining, building: whatever their occupations have by circumstance and choice to be – they write themselves into the nature of things. The trees and hedges, the fields and lanes, the skies over the landscape they have helped to shape, take on something of their humanity. The world of nature is not separate any more. It is made into something different by their qualities. Men actually enter into creation. They are involved in their labour, and in all their arts, in the ongoing creation of the world.

When we have buried the dead, we remember the ways they worked, their jokes, their peculiarities, their characters, the ways in which they lived and enjoyed and endured their fortunes and tragedies. We use their tools, their ingenuities and ideas, after them. In thought and feeling, as in physical fact, we walk the many ways they made. The dead have made the very fabric of our lives. They have entered into us. Their nature is in our flesh and blood and bones, and, in a thousand ways, their senti-ments form part of our spirit. To seek to know ourselves is, therefore, to some extent to seek to know the communities of the past which have made us what we are; and in the complexities of our modern world, with its rapidity of change and the circumstances and pressures which leave us little time for stillness, quietness and reflection, perhaps it is the re-discovery of these bonds of human continuity which we need.

At any rate, in coming gradually, in my own activities, to this savour-ing of our past, it has seemed to me that this now holds a significance for us that goes very deep. It is something more than mere memory. To search our memory, Hume once said, is to discover our identity. It has to do with self-discovery, with spiritual regeneration, with a desire for an honesty of self-recognition, and it is essentially in a movement back to simplicity, to ordinariness, in which its significance lies. There is some-thing in it, too, of a desire to reject the over-reaching, over-sophisticated, over-pretentious claims of modern science, technology and control. My feeling is that we have come to a point of wanting to shed all non-essentials, all falsities. We want only to know what we truly are, where we want to go, how we want to live. The vast framework of human knowledge, even of human society, of 'civilization', has become an im-prisoning cage for us – a Frankenstein kind of master rather than a servant for the realization of our true nature. We are tired of analyzing, managing and controlling the world. We want to get back to a sense of living in a world of wonder which we know, at the heart of us, is there to enjoy.

The strange thing is that this universal human need can only strike roots in localities. The local is the essential ground for the universal. Truth, for each of us, lies in our exploration of what lies on our own doorstep. And this, among many reasons, is one important reason why I love living in East Anglia. More than any other area in England, East Anglia missed the Industrial Revolution. No manufacturing towns – in some ways, despite the improved standards of welfare they brought, savaging both nature and men alike – sprang into being here to sprawl across existing communities distorting, despoiling and destroying them. And therefore there are no acres of burning slag-heaps, under their pall of fumes and smoke, no acres of brick and asphalt houses, streets and slums to be wiped away before life can be reclaimed. Communities here, whether in cities or in villages, go right back a thousand years or more to their very foundations: to early tribesmen, or the Saxons, Norsemen and others who came over the North Sea and set up their homesteads in these well-watered heathlands and forests. Turn over any stone in East Anglia and you find some part of our ancient story. The ancestral link is here, plain to be seen.

The churchyards here are not only elegies; they are history books – and history books saying something of importance in a language which is not 'academic', as other histories are, but familiar to us all.

1 The Unknown Villager

Beneath those rugged elms, that yew-tree's shade,
  Where heaves the turf in many a mould'ring heap,
Each in his narrow cell for ever laid,
  The rude forefathers of the hamlet sleep ...

I began feeling like this in the village of Westleton, in Suffolk – and for
the simple reason, I think, that as I got to know it I got to like it. I
stumbled accidentally across some aspects of its history, and began to
learn and think more about it, but then – as I studied the records –
people began to rise up out of them. Where before I had seen only names
on lists, individual characters began to shake their shoulders and stand
up. It was as though these dead were being awakened, resurrected. They
seemed close, as though they had something to say. And there were
reasons for this.

Besides the historic records, the materials in the county archives, I
began to find all sorts of things in the village itself. In an antique shop,
in a mouldy old chest on a bottom shelf, I found a whole box full of
Victorian photographic plates. Nearby, I also came across many boxes of
magic lantern slides (and the magic lantern itself) which had been
mounted by the photographer who had owned the plates. These slides
gave a pictorial history of the village from about the late 1870s to the
early 1960s – a span of almost a century. The archive records began to be
filled in with details of places, faces and events. Then, as I asked about
these people and events, I discovered that there were still old people in
the village – in their eighties and upwards – who not only remembered
them but who also possessed other photographs, newspaper cuttings and
objects of various kinds which added many other details. Gradually, the
village community and its people came to life.

A church has stood on the same spot in Westleton for a thousand

Westleton churchyard: *stories beneath the turf*

years, and the present building is something like 400 years old. The churchyard is filled with memorials of all kinds: large family vaults covered over with brambles, small stone angels recalling children, and even pre-Victorian 'headstones' made of iron. And there are stones commemorating remarkable and well-known characters. One, for example, tells of June Perry – strange though this name sounds for a man – who was a warrener in Windsor Great Park during the reigns of four sovereigns: George III, George IV, William IV and, of course, Queen Victoria. Another, much more colourful, is Old Buck – William Buck – who was a Crimean veteran, a fact that he never forgot. With scruffy grey whiskers, none too clean, he used to walk round the village with a stick. Irritable and impatient with children and young people who looked slovenly and untidy, he would bark out at them, in military manner, 'Now then, dress yourselves!' or 'Come, come now! As you were!' He took it upon himself to stop children throwing stones and sticks down the village well on the green, and would chase them off with his stick. And he used to stand (or sit) guard on a plot of land he owned with another man: sitting behind the hedge in a small hut that looked like a sentry-box, with a shot-gun across his knees – to scare off the birds. There is a story, too, that on one occasion when Waters Elmy, a young seafaring man,

A Westleton harvest supper gathering, taken in the back yard of The Crown Inn

was at home, Old Buck got so drunk with him in The White Horse (just at the corner of the green) that he was unable to get out of his chair. Waters had to wheel him home in a wheelbarrow, but, though Buck never said a word, he sat bolt upright all the way. And when he died, he was buried near the door of the church with military ceremonial, including a gun-carriage.

The more I went on, the more detailed – and human – the picture became. Soon I was learning the stories of people lying beneath the turf of the churchyard where there were no headstones at all. Those who, on the surface, were totally forgotten, began to come to life. I learned more about more of the people – like the gathering standing outside The Crown Inn about 80–100 years ago. I found out how some of them worked: Billie Smith, the crippled chimney sweep; old Mr Addy Elmy and Reuben Noy, who worked on the roads; Mr Fisk, the wheelwright, choosing and felling timber with his sons and other helpers; and farm labourers, with their new-fangled steam threshing machine which travelled from farm to farm and village to village.

Most of them would gather together for the harvest supper and have their photograph taken in the back yard of The Crown. Stories could still be told about all of them. The man at the end of the bottom row on

The *new-fangled* steam threshing machine: it is possibly Trinity Piffney standing above the sacks of grain

the left of the photograph is Prinny Barker – who was, though he may not look it, a Sunday School teacher. The man three places to the right, pipe in mouth, is Old Munchy Brown – who never stopped chewing (except to smoke!). And the man at the right-hand end of the third row down, wearing what looks like a ten-gallon hat, is 'No-hair Smith', who was a farm labourer at nearby Hinton Farm, and as bald as a coot. Two places to the left of him is 'Scot' Spall, who was quite a character. He was known for poaching – for dealing in pheasants' eggs – and the police once thought they would catch him red-handed by stopping his cart as he drove along the Lowestoft road. But Scot heard about it, got rid of his eggs beforehand, and, in his turn, got ready for them. When they stopped him, he swore passionately that he had no eggs, and pleaded with them whatever else they did, *not* to rummage under his tarpaulin because they would spoil the rhubarb he had carefully stored there. One of the constables laughed, pulled the edge of the sheet back and thrust his hand down hard . . . only to find that he had plunged it, and the sleeve of his uniform, deep into a load of soft manure.

One other fact of great significance emerged in connection with a more tragic incident in Scot's life. His son, at quite a young age, was washed overboard from a trawler at Grimsby and drowned. Unable to leave his

Testament to the anguish of a fishing community: three premature deaths at sea in the Spall families

own work, Scot sent his wife to have his son's body brought home, but, persuaded by others, she allowed him to be buried in Yorkshire. Scot Spall, it is said, never got over this loss and distant burial and left instructions that when he himself died, a memorial to his son should be carved on his own stone. It took me a long time to find the stone with these details, but eventually, I thought, I did. But then, reflecting on the dates, I felt they must surely be too early. So I looked again, just in case there might have been a second similar incident. And, indeed, I did find a second stone, with almost the same story. But again, the dates did not quite fit, and, still searching, I finally did come to Scot Spall's stone itself: and the significance was plain. Nothing, surely, could be a more telling piece of evidence of the typical ordeals endured by the people of a community dependent largely on fishing than these three headstones of three fathers with the same name who had lost their sons at the same age, on the brink of manhood, in the same kind of disaster.

So much in the history of a community – it struck me again – is not sufficiently captured in the 'historical record' of documents and archives. What intrigued me most was all that was *not* in the historical record, and this led me to think particularly about one apparently insignificant man.

Sitting beside Prinny Barker in the harvest supper photograph was a

small man with a broad smile on his face which was like that of a gnome. Who was he?

His name – the old people who told me about him had a struggle to remember his real name – was 'Trinity Piffney'. He was only about four feet high, and a hunchback. He was deformed throughout his life and never any use whatever in ordinary man's work; he was too weak for that. He was, strictly speaking, no real use in the community at all. He was called 'Trinity' (said the old people) because he was such a staunch church-man; a regular attender who never missed any church occasion. And (they thought) he might have had 'Piffney' tacked on because he was for ever here and there, like a puff and dart, all over the village, running errands, chiefly for the vicar. It seems more probable, though, that his nickname was a slight abbreviation of 'Trinity Epiphany' – despite the fact that the running of errands seems to have been all that he did (as well as haunting the village reading room, sprawled out in a chair reading all the newspapers). Whether in winter, when the snow, for all its harshness, made the village look beautiful, or in summer, when the harvest came round, he would be about his errands. It was the only thing he was fit for.

But despite his deformity, despite his 'uselessness', the village found a place for him, the community accepted him as it accepted all others – and he was as happy as a bird. A poor cap, poor clothes, but always a wide grin. Sometimes, too, perhaps he was allowed to help in some occupations. It seems to me likely that it is Trinity Piffney standing on the straw (just above the bags of grain) in the threshing photograph.

His real name was George Bloomfield, and he lived in a small cottage in Mill Street with his mother who had to take in washing to keep him. She, it seems, never went to church: Trinity always went to church alone. She is sitting, in the harvest supper photograph, just over Trinity's left shoulder in the row above him – as tiny as he was. Her name was Mary Ann Bloomfield – *Miss* Mary Ann Bloomfield. Nothing is known about Trinity's father, and when I asked an old lady about this, she said gently, with a touch of reproof, as though there was something improper in my question: 'Well, you know, I don't believe anybody even thought to ask.' But she kept her son by her own hard work, and obviously gave a hand in helping with the harvest supper.

Trinity Piffney, *the Unknown Villager*: he ran errands 'like a puff and dart all over the village'

Old Westleton in
winter

Miss Mary Ann
Bloomfield, Trinity
Piffney's mother

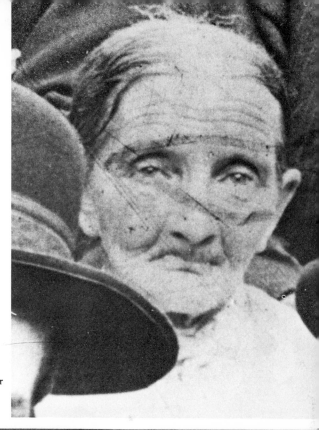

The light-filled interior
of one of Trinity's
favourite spots,
Westleton church

The inside of the church Trinity Piffney loved to attend is simple and beautiful – white, clean, spacious – soaring high up to the roof which, outside, is thatched. In the church there are carved symbols of the two basic occupations of all East Anglian communities – cultivating the land and fishing in the sea; and inside the church, too, are the tombs and plaques commemorating the wealthier and more famous families of the past. But Trinity Piffney does not lie here. He lies outside, under a triangular tongue of turf which is not marked by any stone at all. The 'historical' record knows nothing about it. And nobody knows at all where his mother is.

We are used to thinking of the Unknown Warrior – symbolizing all those unknown soldiers of the past who have preserved our security by giving their lives in war – but we rarely, if ever, think of the 'Unknown Villager', symbolizing all those forgotten labourers of the past whose lives, work and character have gone into the making of our living communities, as they have been, and as they now are. The turf over Trinity Piffney, marked by no stone, is perhaps a symbol with this significance.

2 Promoted to Glory

> Perhaps in this neglected spot is laid
>   Some heart once pregnant with celestial fire;
> Hands, that the rod of empire might have sway'd,
>   Or wak'd to ecstasy the living lyre . . .

It was while wandering round Westleton, looking into the details of Trinity Piffney's life, that I came across another name and another story; the story of a Westleton poet.

From about the turn of the century up to between the two world wars, a blind organ-grinder – Blind Montgomery – used to wander about the village green and along all the lanes and tracks of the country round about, between Aldeburgh, Halesworth and Southwold. He had his poems set up by Southwold Press and sold them for a penny a time. Sometimes the proceeds were for himself, but very often for charity. By great good fortune, I found that his daughter, who still lives in Felixstowe, had kept all his poems. Also, it turned out that he had kept a diary. Walter Scott Montgomery was his name – a literary name if you like.

I was born on the 29th of October, 1867, at 127 Sidney Street, Mile End Road, London. My father was in the East India Company and spent a lot of his time in India. He came home in 1869 when the Cholera was very bad in London, and caught it, and died after a very short illness . . .

His mother died, too, soon after they had moved to Topcroft, a village near Bungay, and from then on he had a rough time of it. He was sent to three different boarding-schools and then off to sea, when he was 16, on the *Spheroid* to St Domingo in the West Indies. He was miserable and tried to run away from the ship whenever it came to port, but the captain kept a close eye on him. They had a hard voyage back, working the pumps all the way to keep the *Spheroid* afloat. But five months later

did my best to get the army there. I left Mr
Clark after I had been with him about five
months because he got drunk so often and
went to work for Mr J Chapman. South
green Southwold. About this time the army
captured the old drill Hall and turned it into
a S.A. Barracks & Capt. Daw opened Southwold
as an outpost but as soon as he farewelled Capt
Dack opened it as a caps & 15 recruits were sworn in
In time I became of age and went to London
to recieve my money I had about £430 I
gave my step sister £100 due to her. I intended
to get married but I seemed very undecided what
to do Harriett felt it her duty to wait for a time
I left my situation which was the worst thing I
could do as I had a very good place, I did not
know when I was well off. I became aquainted
with Mr Frank Swift's Swiss choir and was per-
-suaded to join it which I did going into partnership with Swift a week after. Harriett offered

herself for the work & & was accepted and
became an officer in the Salvation army so we
were parted, I did not care much what I did
& let Swift persuade me into anything as he
liked, I had been two years in Southwold when
I left with the choir I kept a diary from
that time.

26

he was back in Whitechapel, and there he happened to see the Salvation Army. Before long, he was converted, and had joined up.

Montgomery had a lot of jobs in London and then in Ipswich – carting bricks, driving a baker's cart – but then he advertised and got a job with a baker in Southwold. Clearly, however, he was not yet ready to settle down. About this time, he inherited a few hundred pounds and, feeling sick at heart after a lover's tiff with a Southwold girl called Harriet, he was foolishly persuaded to invest a good deal of it in a partnership with a Mr Frank Swift who ran a 'Swiss Choir'. Swift obviously fleeced him. The diary records many 'contributions' of £50, £10, £80 here and there. They travelled down to Kent, giving concerts in halls and on piers, then by boat to Scotland, and then back down to the north country. Montgomery listed 63 towns which they visited, and his record makes good reading: rather like a chronicle of a company of 'strolling players'. But then, in May 1889, an entry says:

Smash. The choir is broke. They have left 15 of us without food or lodgings or money. As soon as Swift was gone, I walked down the road by myself, thinking things over, and wrote the following verses.

The History of Frank Swift's
Royal Swiss Choir

T'was in the town of Spalding
   The Choir's life began,
Frank Swift was its proprietor –
   A swindler's life he ran.

King's Lynn and Norwich were the next
   Towns that they journied through.
What happened next at Lowestoft
   I will relate to you.

Swift fell in with a foolish lad
   Who had a little coin,
So with false words persuaded him
   His Choir at once to join.

His name it was Montgomery,
   The agent he came round,
Persuading him to pay a fee
   Of five and twenty pound.

The Choir performed in Beccles,
   And then to Norwich went,
Montgomery joined the Choir here,
   A step he does repent.

> Frank Swift, with artful oily tongue,
>   Montgomery got round,
> Till he went into partnership
>   By paying eighty pound ...

Well, the ballad goes on for 34 verses in all, telling the tale of the choir's travels, performances, lodging-houses, variable food, and a long list of disasters. Three other brief quotations are enough to indicate his tone. This, for example, is how the choir had to depart from Scotland!

> Then quietly back to Aberdeen,
>   And quick on board the boat,
> Detectives then we gave the slip
>   And safely were afloat.
>
> We dared not come by passenger,
>   But on a cattle ship
> Then back to dear old England
>   We had a roughish trip.
>
> When in Newcastle we landed
>   We were glad to get to bed
> For we had spent an awful night –
>   Sea-sick and nearly dead.

It is interesting to note, too, that Frank Swift had, at least on some occasions, to pay for his misdemeanours:

> We then arrived in Otley,
>   And t'was but the 2nd day,
> When Frank Swift was arrested
>   And taken safe away.
>
> For giving out dishonoured cheques
>   He to Pontefract was taken,
> But afterwards in Wakefield jail
>   He spent a short vacation.

and, also, that not even he and his 'artful, oily tongue' could fool the people of Manchester:

> And then we went to Manchester,
>   Old Swift here meets his match –
> For with these false dishonoured cheques
>   *These* Folk he cannot catch!
>
> For when we reached the Hall that day
>   The gas they would not light
> Unless the hard cash was paid down ...
>   So Swift shut up that night!

So much for the hard-headed people of Lancashire! Ultimately defeated, and penniless, Montgomery tramped back home from Runcorn, sleeping in haycocks and straw-stacks; it took him eight days but he got back, at last, to the bakery and the Salvation Army at Southwold. And there he got married and started a family. He worked hard, often from 5 o'clock in the morning, sometimes all night getting ready for Bank Holidays and sports days. Many entries in his diary just say: 'Usual work – very busy – tired.' 'Usual work – don't feel at all well.' 'Usual work – feel very queer.' And he obviously regarded nine shillings a week as a very good week's pay. Increasingly, too, he was busy with Salvation Army meetings and continually talked about 'having souls':

Blind Montgomery's donkey and organ, with friend Snowden on the left and
Montgomery on the right

Sunday, 17th September: Harvest Thanksgiving, good day, we had one soul in
the morning, a young man just out of Ipswich Jail, just done 18 months hard.
He has written to his mother and promised to go home. His home is at Mitcham,
Surrey.

Early in the morning, Montgomery would be off from the Southwold
Bakery, with a tray of bread on his head, to walk down over the common
and the footbridge to Walberswick. Walking meant nothing to him. He
would walk from Southwold to Saxmundham for a meeting, which would
take him only 20 minutes short of four hours. But then – blindness
struck him. For many years after that, he lived in a small cottage in
Westleton – just a bit further up Mill Street from Trinity Piffney and
his mother. He started going round the villages, helped by his son Clif-
ford, with an accordion. Then the people clubbed together to buy him
an organ and a donkey, and sometimes he was helped by a friend of his,
Snowden, who himself had had polio. The leg supported by the wooden
leg in the photograph was not an amputated but a withered leg. Sometimes the donkey could not be used and Montgomery's daughters helped
him to pull the organ round, often having to take off their boots or shoes

Britannia's Greatest Soldier.

—✠—

In Loving Memory of
FIELD - MARSHALL LORD KITCHENER,
K.G., K.P., G.C.B., O.M., G.C.S.I., G.C.M.G., G.C.I.E.

Who was drowned off the Orkneys, June 5th, 1916,
H.M.S. Hampshire, on which he was travelling, striking a mine
and sinking in ten minutes.

The highest tribute earth can give each Briton's tongue shall tell,
He lived and died for England's sake, he did his duty well.

Our Empire now is plunged in grief, we mourn a hero true,
A gallant soul, our army's chief, his time and talents too
Devoted were to country dear, no loyal heart more bolder,
But now alas he is no more, Britannia's greatest soldier.

He died not on the battlefield, his sword was in its sheath,
The good ship Hampshire ploughed the wave, her smoke in curling wreath
Was from the Orkney Islands seen, the squally breeze blew colder,
With Kitchener and Staff on board, Britannia's greatest soldier.

En route for Petrograd was he on mission for the war,
The watchers gazing out to sea with horror clearly saw
The good ship suddenly go down, no human power could hold her,
Beneath those cruel ice cold waves with England's greatest soldier.

The ship, alas, had struck a mine laid by the devilish hun,
Appalling is this fiendish crime, but England's day shall come
For retribution, swift and sure, e'er they be grown much older
May over-take them and avenge Britannia's greatest soldier.

For five-and-forty years he served with never-failing zeal,
His laurels won he well deserved, our foes his vengence feel,
A stern disciplinarian he was our army's moulder,
Weeping, Britannia mourns alas her grandest, ablest soldier.

Well may the brutal hun rejoice and o'er his murder gloat,
They dreaded him upon the field, they feared him when afloat,
His flashing eye, his marshal mien, would make their hearts grow colder,
The tyrant filled with craven fear at Engand's greatest soldier

He fought and fell for England's sake, his duty nobly done,
He crushed the mighty Madhi's power and would have crushed the hun,
Had not the dastard murderers crept with blackest heart, none colder,
Assassinating him they feared the whole world's greatest soldier.

Brave warrior chief! his fame shall live his gallant deeds shall tell,
The greatest tribute earth can give—he did his duty well,
His name shall blaze on history's page when all our hearts are colder,
Our children's children learn of him, Britannia's greatest soldier.

Unitedly our Empire mourns the hero's loss deploring,
A nation dear mingles its tear with loved ones weeping for him,
But far beyond all earthly strife where the faithful ne'er grow older
Lives Kitchener once of Khartoum, and England's greatest soldier.

By W. S. Montgomery,
Blind Organ Grinder,
Westleton.

✠　　In Loving Memory of　　✠

OUR BELOVED KING EDWARD VII.

Born November 9th, 1841.
Became King January 1901.
Died May 6th, 1910.

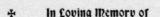

Alas his glorious reign is o'er, Britannia mourns her King,
Throughout the realm the flag is lowered, the tolling bell doth ring,
And every loyal Briton's heart is filled with grief to-day,
Our Royal Sovereign loved by all from earth has passed away.

Our King endeared himself to all, we loved him as a lad,
When Prince of Wales his kindly acts oft made his people glad,
And when to place upon his brow, the royal crown they bring,
The country rang throughout with joy and cried "God Save the King."

His glorious reign, although so short, has been a time of peace,
For 'twas at his accession the Transvaal War did cease,
And everything seemed prosperous, the sky looked bright and clear,
And each one prayed our King might reign for many a 'ppy year.

But he is dead! the mournful news has spread throughout the land,
Cast gloom and sorrow everywhere there's grief on every hand,
But nine short years King Edward reigned, the nations tears doth fall,
So suddenly was called to rest beloved and mourned by all.

The Royal Household's plunged in woe, sad was the parting scene,
We pray God comfort those bereaved oh bles our widowed Queen,
Their refuge Thou hast ever been we bow before Thy will,
Console our Royal Family and be their refuge still.

　　　　　　　　By W. S. MONTGOMERY,
　　　　　　　　　　　　Blind Organ Grinder

and stockings and manhandle the organ through water and over the uneven beds of streams. They pulled and pushed it for miles around – Aldeburgh, Yoxford, Wenhaston, Halesworth, Walberswick, Southwold – an area back from the coast with a radius of about 12 miles.

But Walter Scott Montgomery was always cheerful. He enjoyed his life. People knew his family as a closely united one, pulling together in meeting their difficulties, and used to look forward to his rounds. Little girls used to dance to his music in the streets when he came. And if Blind Montgomery had lost all his money when he left Frank Swift and his choir, he had found another activity – writing verses. Soon his penny poems were well-known all over the area and, taken altogether now, they are almost a history in themselves.

Such patriotic poems were brought to the attention of kings and queens, and were, in time, royally acknowledged. Walter Scott Montgomery's long history of verses included the death and coronation celebrations of several reigns.

" DEFEND THEY RYGHT."

TUNE. "Wait for the Waggon."

There is a very ancient borough,
A little seaside town,
Where Mr. Bumble and Dame Fashion
From somewhere have dropped down,
And with old Doctor Crush-em-all
Intend at once to try
To rule the place and have declared
Old customs here must die.

Chorus – Lift high the banner!
Lift high the banner!
Lift high the banner!
Defend, defend they Ryght!

They won the sympathy and help
Of the honoured, worthy Mayor,
Whose latest move has been to try
And shift the Chartered Fair,
He called a Council Meeting,
And there it was agreed
By a very small majority,
To shift the Fair indeed.

That never more upon South Green
They'd be allowed to come,
But on the Common, out of town,
He'd find them lots of room,
And if they should refuse to move,
He said he'd not proclaim,
But when the Burgesses heard this,
To him they did exclaim :

TUNE. —" Following in father's footsteps."

Chorus – Come! follow in your father's footsteps,
Come! follow your dear old dad,
Who for thirty years proclaimed the Fair,
No stupid scruples had,
Upheld the ancient custom,
And a treat the children had,
Don't bar the road but don your robe,
And follow your dear old dad.

The Mayor, alas! proved obstinate,
And a score brave bobbies bold,
To form a cordon 'cross the path,
And bar the streets were told,
But the showman quickly cleared the way,
Before the engine's track,
The Burgesses all cried with glee,
As the men in blue stepped back.

TUNE. —" The Bogie Man."

Hi! hi! hi! here comes the Chartered Fair,
The organ and the roundabouts,
The swinging-boats were there.
Look! look! look! ye gallant men in blue,
You'd better get back from the engine's track,
Or else they'll mangle you.

Next morning in the Market Place,
En masse the folk did come,
To hear the Chartered Fair proclaimed,
All looking for the fun.
The gallant band came marching up,
Led by a banner bright—
Enscribèd with the Township's Arms,
And read " Defend they Ryght."

Conspicuous by his absence then,
The Mayor did not appear,
But when the Town Clerk shewed himself,
The Burgesses did cheer :
He read the Proclamation
And a Burgess did proclaim
That on South Green the Chartered Fair
For ever should remain.

TUNE. —" Rule Britannia."

So forward justice, we claim our ancient right,
And for the victory we mean to fight.

By W. S. MONTGOMERY,
Blind Organ Grinder.

But he also wrote poems about striking local events and incidents which attracted attention. Very frequently in this part of the world, there were wrecks at sea and lifeboat disasters, and Montgomery sold poems about all of these to raise money for the dependants left behind.

Perhaps most enjoyable, however, are the poems in which he attacks Southwold's Town Council for wasting money, and the snobs from outside who retire to the town thinking they can run everything over the heads, and the long established rights, of the local inhabitants.

But it must be remembered that Montgomery was blind – easy though it is to forget it, with the evidence of his unflagging energy and unending output of verses. Every now and then, some of his sheets could not be sold for charity but had to contain his own requests, like this:

Kind Friends,
    I am endeavouring by the sale of these verses to raise what I can to get my Organ overhauled and marking with fresh tunes. Thanking you sincerely for your assistance in the past.
                    I am, Yours gratefully,
                        W. S. MONTGOMERY, Blind Organ-Grinder.

And, of course, all his verses had to be dictated and taken down by his wife or one of his daughters. Here are the first two verses of 'Little Annie and Her Collecting Box', exactly as they were taken down.

1   Little Annie and her collecting box
Twas at a village chapel and the children from . school
Had each got a collecting box as often was the rule
Collecting for the gospel work in foreign lands away
To teach heathens, to kneel te images of wood and stone to pray.

2
A missionary once a year round to the chapel came,
and at the meeting would read . . . what each box could contain
And each one at that Sunday school would do their very best
To see who could collect the most so out do the rest.

Many verses later, the poem ends with Little Annie confronted by a row of coins – from a farthing to a sovereign – and a £5 note laid out on the table by an artful squire. Annie selects the sovereign and asks him, much to his delight and approval, to 'wrap it up in the piece of paper' (the £5 note), thus winning a large prize for her collection.

Montgomery's poems would now make a very thick volume, but when they were written, sung and sold, they formed a continuous entertainment at the doors of houses, on the commons and greens of villages, and in the streets. And though he is still remembered partly as a Westleton man, partly as a Southwold man, Blind Montgomery is not buried in either place. A Salvation Army man to the end, and helped to the end by his wife, he left very definite instructions. His diary says:

In case of my death it is my wish that I be buried in the nearest cemetary by my present Corps of the Salvation Army, I wish for a milliatary funeral according to the Rules & Regulations of the Salvation Army

signed W. S. Montgomery

His family respected his wish, and his grave is in the cemetery at Halesworth, engraved in true Salvation Army manner: 'Walter Scott Montgomery: Promoted to Glory'. I myself, however, cannot help seeing him, still, on the edge of Westleton Heath, going through the gorse bushes from one village to another, his music going with him, some of his best-remembered tunes and poems under his arm.

Blind Montgomery in Salvation Army uniform (see page 36)

3 Mysterious Ways

Hard by yon wood, now smiling as in scorn,
　Mutt'ring his wayward fancies he would rove;
Now drooping, woeful-wan, like one forlorn,
　Or craz'd with care, or cross'd in hopeless love...

*　*　*

Large was his bounty, and his soul sincere,
　Heaven did a recompense as largely send:
He gave to mis'ry (all he had) a tear,
　He gain'd from heav'n, ('twas all he wish'd) a friend.

No farther seek his merits to disclose,
　Or draw his frailties from their dread abode
(There they alike in trembling hope repose),
　The bosom of his Father and his God.

Thinking about poetry, the glory of it and the way in which it is often made out of the stuff of adversity, led me straight away to a churchyard I knew at East Dereham. Blind Montgomery was a local Victorian 'penny poet', struggling through the poverty of the nineteenth century (made much worse by his blindness) into our own time. He died two years after the end of the Second World War. But among the quiet trees in East Dereham churchyard lies one of the greatest, if one of the quietest, poets of the eighteenth century; William Cowper, a poet with as great a degree of personal integrity as any poet in any century.

Strangely, Cowper is not well known, except for his story of John Gilpin's ride, and yet he was criticizing the tendencies and attitudes of the new commercialized industrial society long before the Romantics – Wordsworth, Shelley, Byron and others – and, often, on much the same ground. Indeed, many of Cowper's lines have become common English expressions without it being realized that they have come from him – phrases like: '... the cups that cheer, but not inebriate', 'Variety's the

East Dereham churchyard: William Cowper lies beneath the quiet trees

very spice of life', 'God made the country and man made the town', and 'England, for all thy faults, I love thee still'.

In East Dereham church a magnificent stained-glass window commemorates Cowper, a man who all his life was gentle, quiet, withdrawn, unbalanced and disturbed, timid to the point of unbearable anxiety. He was born in Berkhamstead, with some intimate physical – probably sexual – deformity, which ravaged him as a child, and made his school-life (he was sent to two boarding-schools before going to Westminster) a misery, a torture, from bullying. This childhood agony was the beginning of a terrible religious insanity, when he believed himself to have been

William Cowper: poet of suffering and gentleness

damned – cut off for ever from God, never to have fulfilment. His mother died when he was six and he needed what he had never had enough of – love. He needed it, too, in adult life, when he was never able to experience its fulfilment. All his life he suffered periods of deep, ungovernable depression, in one of which, eventually, he died. There was never much relief from mental and spiritual stress.

But despite this suffering, this gentleness, consider the forthrightness, the outspokenness, of the following lines, written at a time when slavery was taken for granted by many:

> To purify their wine some people bleed
> A lamb into the barrel, and succeed;
> No nostrum, planters say, is half so good
> To make fine sugar, as a *negro's* blood.
> Now *lambs* and *negroes* both are harmless things,
> And thence perhaps this wondrous virtue springs.
> 'Tis in the blood of innocence alone . . .
> Good cause why planters never try their own.

> Slavery! Virtue dreads it as her grave!
> Canst thou, and honoured with a Christian name,
> Buy what is woman born, and feel no shame;
> Trade in the blood of innocence, and plead
> Expedience as a warrant for the deed?

That is hardly insane, or timid. There was nothing quiet, gentle, withdrawn about Cowper as far as social justice was concerned; and, in his day, not many were criticizing English society like this.

He had tried to follow his father's wish and the family tradition of going into the Law. He became a member of the Inner Temple but when he had to face a simple interview by a committee of the House of Lords, connected with a minor clerical job, his terror was such as to drive him to attempt suicide. The truth was that he was crippled for coming to terms with the demands of the ordinary world which most of us have to bear.

It was at Olney, in Bedfordshire, that he finally found the friendship, retreat and protection that he needed. He had gone to live with a Reverend Unwin, his wife Mary and their family, and when Unwin died, they were given the use of a house at Olney (which is now a museum, containing many of Cowper's possessions). Here he worked closely with a Reverend Newton, devoting himself to religious work. He still suffered long periods of melancholy, but it was out of these very sufferings that many lines were written that we now know intimately:

> God moves in a mysterious way
> His wonders to perform;
> He plants his footsteps in the sea,
> And rides upon the storm.

> Deep in unfathomable mines
> Of never failing skill
> He treasures up his bright designs,
> And works his sov'reign will.

> Ye fearful saints, fresh courage take;
> The clouds ye so much dread
> Are big with mercy, and shall break
> In blessings on your head.

Despite their conviction of God's irrevocable will for himself, Cowper could still write like that.

But the way for him, and for Mary Unwin – now his closest companion – was only one of decline. Later, when they both had to be cared for, they moved to Norfolk, near friends, and finally to East Dereham. Cowper tried to deal with his madness in all sorts of ways – keeping hares as pets, for example, and he was quite the biological observer!

I describe these animals as having each a character of his own. Such they were in fact, and their countenances were so expressive of their character, that, when I looked on the face of each, I immediately knew which it was ... The sportsman little knows what amiable creatures he persecutes, of what gratitude they are capable, what enjoyment they have of life, and that – impressed as they seem with a peculiar dread of man – it is only because man gives them peculiar cause for it.

He even had special seals made for them, carrying the names of the three hares – Puss and Bess who were reasonably tamed, and Tiney, who never was!

> Old Tiney, surliest of his kind,
> Who, nursed with tender care,
> And to domestic bounds confined,
> Was still a wild Jack-Hare.
>
> Though daily from my hand he took
> His pittance every night,
> He did it with a jealous look,
> And, when he could, would bite.
>
> I kept him for his humour's sake,
> For he would oft beguile
> My heart of thoughts that made it ache;
> And force me to a smile.

Friends encouraged his poetry, but out of the gentle subjects they suggested – 'The Sofa', 'The Task', 'The Winter Evening' – came forthright social criticism. Cowper saw the distastefulness of the commercial and industrial society growing up all round him:

> Man in society is like a flower
> Blown in its native bed: 'tis there alone
> His faculties, expanded in full bloom,
> Shine out; there only reach their proper use.
> But man, associated and leagued with man
> For interest sake, or swarming into clans
> Beneath one head for purposes of war...
> Contracts defilement not to be endured.

> Hence chartered boroughs are such public plagues;
> And burghers, men immaculate perhaps
> In all their private functions, once combined,
> Become a loathsome body, only fit
> For dissolution, hurtful to the main.
> Hence merchants, unimpeachable of sin
> Against the charities of domestic life,
> Incorporated seem at once to lose
> Their nature; and disclaiming all regard
> For mercy and the common rights of man,
> Build factories with blood, conducting trade
> At the sword's point, and dying the white robe
> Of innocent commercial justice – red.

Furthermore, he believed that a deterioration of society, culture, taste and character was bound to follow from the emphasis on wealth and social status and the spreading fever of competition for these:

> The course of human things from good to ill,
> From ill to worse, is fatal, never fails;
> Increase of power begets increase of wealth;
> Wealth luxury, and luxury excess;
> Excess, the scrofulous and itchy plague,
> That seizes first the opulent, descends
> To the next rank contagious, and in time
> Taints downwards all the graduated scale
> Of order, from the chariot to the plough.

Scathing criticisms of commerce, war, slavery, education, the press – of much that was thought to constitute 'progress' – poured out of him. He attacked everything that was superficial and inhuman, and some of this social criticism was well-considered and profound, and deserves notice. Here are a few of Cowper's comments on 'education' and the 'schools' which were replacing private tuition. They would make him a good contributor to a sound Black Paper, and place him quite firmly among the 'de-schoolers' – 200 years before their time.

First, he thought, the emphasis on the ends of education had gone wrong: social 'accomplishments', not truth, knowledge and qualities of mind, judgment and character, were the things desired:

> Accomplishments have taken virtue's place,
> And wisdom falls before exterior grace;
> We slight the precious kernel of the stone,
> And toil to polish its rough coat alone.
> A just deportment, manners graced with ease,
> Elegant phrase, and figure formed to please,
> Are qualities that seem to comprehend

> Whatever parents, guardians, schools intend;
> Hence an unfurnished and a listless mind,
> Though busy, trifling; empty, though refined;
> Hence all that interferes, and dares to clash
> With indolence and luxury, is trash.
> Learning itself, received into a mind
> By nature weak, or viciously inclined,
> Serves but to lead philosophers astray,
> Where children would with ease discern the way.
> And of all arts sagacious dupes invent,
> To cheat themselves and gain the world's assent,
> The worst is – scripture warped from its intent.

It is interesting to see that, a good religious man, Cowper could not stand much precious theology, and, in general, he had not much time for the 'socially acceptable' clergy of his time. But what he chiefly lamented, in education, was the loss of the qualities of discipline, in both mind and character:

> In colleges and halls, in ancient days,
> When learning, virtue, piety and truth,
> Were precious, and inculcated with care,
> There dwelt a sage called Discipline. His head,
> Not yet by time completely silvered o'er,
> Bespoke him past the bounds of freakish youth,
> But strong for service still, and unimpaired.
> His eye was meek and gentle, and a smile
> Played on his lips; and in his speech was heard
> Paternal sweetness, dignity, and love.
> The occupation dearest to his heart
> Was to encourage goodness. He would stroke
> The head of modest and ingenuous worth,
> That blushed at its own praise, and press the youth
> Close to his side that pleased him. Learning grew
> Beneath his care a thriving, vigorous, plant;
> The mind was well informed, the passions held
> Subordinate, and diligence was choice ...

But:

> ... Discipline at length,
> O'erlooked and unemployed, fell sick and died.
> Then study languished, emulation slept,
> And virtue fled; the schools became a scene
> Of solemn farce, where ignorance in stilts,
> His cap well lined with logic not his own,
> With parrot tongue performed the scholar's part,
> Proceeding soon a graduated dunce.
> Then compromise had place, and scrutiny

> Became stone blind; precedence went in truck,
> And he was competent whose purse was so.
> A dissolution of all bonds ensued;
> The curbs invented for the mulish mouth
> Of head-strong youth were broken; bars and bolts
> Grew rusty by disuse; and massy gates
> Forgot their office, opening with a touch;
> Till gowns at length are found mere masquerade,
> The tassled cap and the spruce band a jest,
> A mockery of the world!

What Cowper would think of modern schools and universities can be imagined – the nature of his judgment can be seen from his criticism of schools in his own time:

> Oh barbarous! wouldest thou with a Gothic hand
> Pull down the schools – what! – all the schools i' the land;
> Or throw them up to livery-nags and grooms,
> Or turn them into shops and auction rooms?
> A captious question, sir, (and your's is one)
> Deserves an answer similar, or none.
> Wouldest thou, possessor of a flock, employ
> (Apprized that he is such) a careless boy,
> And feed him well, and give him handsome pay,
> Merely to sleep, and let them run astray?
> Survey our schools and colleges, and see
> A sight not much unlike my simile.
> From education, as the leading cause,
> The public character its colour draws;
> Thence the prevailing manners take their cast,
> Extravagant or sober, loose or chaste.
> And, though I would not advertise them yet,
> Nor write on each – This Building to be Let,
> Unless the world were all prepared to embrace
> A plan well worthy to supply their place;
> Yet, backward as they are, and long have been,
> To cultivate and keep the MORALS clean,
> (Forgive the crime) I wish them, I confess,
> Or better managed, or encouraged less.

The gentle judgments of the gentle William Cowper. He had one particular hatred, too – the popular press, which brought everything down to the lowest possible level:

> How shall I speak thee, or thy power address,
> Thou god of our idolatry, the press?
> By thee religion, liberty, and laws,
> Exert their influence, and advance their cause;
> By thee worse plagues than Pharaoh's land befel,

> Diffused, make earth the vestibule of hell;
> Thou fountain, at which drink the good and wise;
> Thou ever-bubbling spring of endless lies;
> Like Eden's dread probationary tree,
> Knowledge of good and evil is from thee.
> No wild enthusiast ever yet could rest,
> Till half mankind were like himself possessed.
> Philosophers, who darken and pour out
> Eternal truth by everlasting doubt;
> Church quacks, with passions under no command,
> Who fill the world with doctrines contraband,
> Discoverers of they know not what, confined
> Within no bounds – the blind that lead the blind;
> To streams of popular opinion drawn,
> Deposit in those shallows all their spawn.
> The wriggling fry soon fill the creeks around,
> Poisoning the waters where their swarms abound.
> Scorned by the nobler tenants of the flood,
> Minnows and gudgeons gorge th'unwholesome food.

Again, 'Church quacks' as well as others came in for a drubbing. William Cowper, from the quiet of his sofa, was one of the greatest poets and most discerning social critics of the eighteenth century. And his own estimation of the direction in which true values lay was always constant, sound and clear:

> He is the happy man, whose life ev'n now
> Shows somewhat of that happier life to come;
> Who, doomed to an obscure but tranquil state,
> Is pleased with it, and, were he free to choose,
> Would make his fate his choice ...
> Ask him what trophies he has raised,
> Or what achievements of immortal fame
> He purposes, and he shall answer – None.
> His warfare is within. There unfatigued
> His fervent spirit labours. There he fights,
> And there obtains fresh triumphs o'er himself,
> And never-withering wreaths; compared with which
> The laurels that a Caesar reaps are weeds.

Yet his own personal life was doomed to trouble and decline. Sitting together, sharing their problems, Mary Unwin and Cowper grew closer. They became engaged to be married – but, at once, his insanity came on again. And in the last few years of her life, Mary herself suffered several strokes, one of which completely changed her nature. Instead of sympathizing with Cowper and caring for him, she became demanding, tyrannizing over him. Watching her fade was, for him, an added agony:

The twentieth year is well-nigh past,
Since first our sky was overcast;
Ah would that this might be the last!
                    My Mary!

Thy spirits have a fainter flow,
I see thee daily weaker grow –
'Twas my distress that brought thee low,
                    My Mary!

Thy needles, once a shining store,
For my sake restless heretofore,
Now rust disus'd and shine no more,
                    My Mary!

But well thou playd'st the housewife's part
And all thy threads with magic art
Have wound themselves about this heart,
                    My Mary!

Thy silver locks, once auburn bright,
Are still more lovely in my sight
Than golden beams of orient light,
                    My Mary!

Partakers of the sad decline,
Thy hands their little force resign;
Yet gently pressed, press gently mine,
                    My Mary!

And then I feel that still I hold
A richer store ten thousandfold
Than misers fancy in their gold,
                    My Mary!

And still to love, though prest with ill,
In wintry age to feel no chill,
With me is to be lovely still,
                    My Mary!

When, at last, Mary died, Cowper could not and would not believe
that she was dead. His friend, Johnny Johnson, whose family lived nearby
at Mattishall, was reading to him at the time. The news was brought
downstairs to Johnson by a maidservant, and gradually he broke it to
Cowper. Cowper seemed not to realize, and then, in terror, denied it
– having a fear that she would be buried alive, and that the fault would
be his.

Mary Unwin was buried at night, by torchlight, and now lies under
a stone in the north aisle of Dereham church.

Some of Cowper's possessions – quite apart from those in the Olney
museum – remain. His descendants live near Newmarket and there I
was able to see the seals he had made for his pet hares, the curious

Mary Unwin: '*all thy threads with magic art Have wound themselves about this heart, My Mary!*'

Orchard Side, Olney, the Unwins' home: as it appeared when Cowper lived there

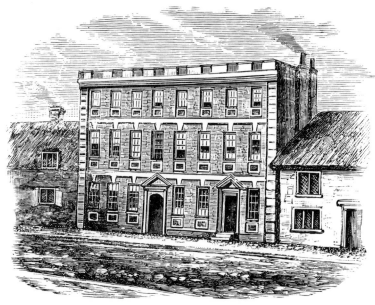

The memorial window to Cowper in East Dereham church

turban-type cap that he is shown wearing in his portrait, some netting that he made as one method of calming the moods of his insanity, and, of course, his books.

The house where Cowper and Mary lived in East Dereham still exists but is changed. One half of it has been made into a chapel, the other into a self-service store. At the back is a large concreted car-park. Only one thing of Cowper's remains, looking down on the modern scene – the copper beech that once looked down on Cowper and Mary in their garden.

Cowper himself lies inside Dereham church under the commemorative window showing all the important elements of his life – his hares, his small summer-house at Olney, his quiet retired life and his poetry – side by side with his religion. Cowper once wrote of Dr Johnson:

> Oh man immortal by a double prize:
> By fame on earth, by glory in the skies.

It could well have been written about himself. Out of a life which was heavily burdened from the beginning by an agony of spirit which could not, by any normal responses and any normal way of life, be borne, a glory was certainly accomplished.

It was while standing under Cowper's window that I realized the underlying thread of feeling which had led me to move from Trinity Piffney to Blind Montgomery to William Cowper – what it was that had linked them together in my mind. Trinity Piffney, who was 'useless' and never created anything but a dimension of gladness in his village; Blind Montgomery, who dictated 'penny poems' out of his darkness, touring the countryside with his hurdy-gurdy music, often for charity; and William Cowper, who made a literature of beauty, wisdom and compassion out of his insanity ... all three had savage burdens to bear. Their humanity was irrevocably diminished; it could never possibly be complete. And yet – in one important way – deformed, blind, insane, they were not. More than others, they had the eye that can see. They loved this world. Despite all their adversity, through all their tragedy – perhaps, in part, even because of it – they sensed something more. And certainly they contributed much to the quality of life of their communities.

No matter how complicated our society has become, here – in the elegies of their country churchyards – they are still at the roots of it, and perhaps have something to say to us now. 'Promoted to Glory' says Blind Montgomery's gravestone. Well, perhaps. But to my mind their glory is here.

4 A National Scandal

Some village Hampden, that, with dauntless breast,
    The little tyrant of the fields withstood,
Some mute inglorious Milton here may rest,
    Some Cromwell guiltless of his country's blood.

Th' applause of list'ning senates to command,
    The threats of pain and ruin to despise,
To scatter plenty o'er a smiling land,
    And read their history in a nation's eyes,

Their lot forbad: nor circumscrib'd alone
    Their growing virtues, but their crimes confined
Forbad to wade thro' slaughter to a throne,
    And shut the gates of mercy on mankind,

Two country churchyards – one at Akenham, one at Claydon – stand just a mile away from each other across the meadows in the sleepy Suffolk countryside a few miles outside Ipswich. It is hard to see what they could possibly have to do with 'little tyrants', 'village Hampdens' or 'shutting the gates of mercy on mankind'; and to talk here about the massive national problems of the nineteenth century or the far-reaching effects of the Industrial Revolution would seem completely out of place. Yet I want to tell you a story of nationwide significance which was lost for a hundred years, and which began here. The way in which it came to light seemed a complete accident.

    I was enjoying a long, dark winter's day, just before Christmas, rummaging through the back shed of an antique shop in Southwold. Among the books, albums and papers strewn all over the floor, piled on shelves, heaped into baskets, I came across an unusual black book. It is on my desk now – about 17 inches long, 12 inches wide, very slender, bound in poor black cloth, faded, stained and torn a little at the corners and along the spine. It turned out to be an old 'day journal' of the 1870s

Claydon: the Reverend George Drury's parish church

Akenham churchyard, the setting for ecclesiastical 'scandal'

– a label on the front saying that it had belonged to Joseph Thurston, an Ipswich 'cabinet maker, etc' of 42, The Buttermarket. Ornamented here and there with pictures of the latest iron bedsteads, the pages contained Mr Thurston's daily transactions – despatching eight pillows to Mr Moberley, London (by Pickfords & Co.); ordering wallpaper; complaining about deliveries ('... I find you call it a 3 ft Bedstead, but the Bedstead measures but 2 ft 6, or do you measure the entire width of Cornice?'). Every item was entered diligently, meticulously, with dates, numbers and page references, by a sharp-pointed metal pen and in an ink now turned brown. But besides being a cabinet maker, Mr Thurston was obviously a man passionately interested in church affairs, especially in the struggles between the Established Church and (it seemed) allcomers – Dissenters, farmers and all other groups in the community. When his book had ended its days as a business journal, Mr Thurston had used it for collecting newspaper-cuttings. Almost every page was pasted over with pieces (still carefully dated) on issues as large as 'Tithes', 'The Condition of the Church of England in Wales', 'The State Church', and as small as 'Church Troubles in Little Stonham'. But, in all these yellow pages of the nineteenth century, one title caught my eye. It was cut from the *East Anglian Daily Times*, 26 August 1878.

BURIAL SCANDAL AT AKENHAM.

A PASSAGE OF ARMS BETWEEN REV. GEORGE DRURY AND REV. WICKHAM TOZER.

From the *East Anglian Daily Times*.
Aug 16 26 — 1878

About midway between the Whitton and the Henley Roads, and about half a mile from both these highways, is the very small hamlet called Akenham. On rising ground, and at sufficient elevation to make it observable from a considerable distance, is the parish church of Akenham. There are not half a dozen houses visible at any one point in the village, and the number of inhabitants can scarcely be more than from 50 to 100, and we doubt very much whether there are anything like so many as that. The church is a very comely looking building—at a distance.

Clergymen at war! It sounded intriguing. And it was in this article that the story of the Akenham Burial Case began. It was reported like this:

About midway between the Whitton and the Henley Roads and about half a mile from these highways is the parish church of Akenham ... If you leave the bridle way and ascend the hill on which it stands, you must be painfully impressed with the fact that the sacred edifice and its surroundings are grievously neglected ... the graveyard is a perfect wilderness – and in the building, cobwebs in profusion, dead birds and dirt in abundance, convince us that it has never been swept for months, if for years ...

The incumbent of this notable village church is the Rev George Drury – FIRM FATHER GEORGE – the well-known rector of the adjoining parish of Claydon – who might often be seen taking a pleasant airing in its vicinity ...

A few days ago, a working man – Edward Ramsey in the employ of Mr Gooding of Akenham Hall – lost a child, Joseph, who was just two years old. Both parents being Baptists, the child was never baptised.

Ipswich is four miles from Akenham, and as there is neither a cemetery nor chapel graveyard nearer, application was made to have it buried in the consecrated ground of the parish church. Mr Drury, on learning that the child had not been baptised, peremptorily refused it burial in the consecrated ground, but gave permission for it to be buried behind the church in ground reserved for still-born infants, on condition that no religious service was performed within the graveyard ...

Mrs Ramsey, visiting the churchyard with a friend to choose a place for her son's grave, was also told by the sexton that 'this was when parents felt the rub of not having had their children baptised' – and that her boy would have to be 'buried like a dog.' Mr Gooding, a kindhearted employer, at once arranged for a short service to be held before the interment, in front of the church gate, in the meadow occupied by Mr Smith of Rise Hall, who is church-warden. They and the dissenting minister – Rev Wickham Tozer – arrived some ten or fifteen minutes early on the day of the funeral. Firm Father George was pacing the graveyard attired in indescribable petticoats and inconceivable headgear. That looked ominous. Both of the reverend gentlemen must have felt that there was something threatening in the air, for they paced up and down their respective paths, the one inside and the other outside the church boundaries with a defiant air that reminded us of two game birds pluming themselves for a brush. At length the humble procession arrived. Before the corpse had been lifted from the cart, the sexton, primed for the occasion, went up to the father of the child and requested that the corpse might be conveyed immediately to the grave and they could hold the service after it was buried, in the meadow outside the yard ...

No notice was taken by the father or his friends, and the coffin was placed on the ground in front of the churchyard gate. The friends gathered round it and Mr Tozer commenced reading appropriate passages of scripture ...

So the newspaper narrative went on; but the dialogue that then took place during the service by the gate developed like this. The Rev. Wickham Tozer was reading his chosen verses: 'Now the days of David drew nigh, that he should die; and he charged Solomon, his son, saying: I go the way of all the earth: be thou strong therefore, and show thyself a man ...'

But at this point, Father Drury sailed out of the gate in full regalia and planted himself very close to Tozer, conspicuously facing all the mourners. His manner was testy and impatient, and he interrupted Tozer

Left: A contemporary caricature of Firm Father George
Right: The dissenting Wickham Tozer: 'a man of strong character'

irritably: 'The time for this funeral was five o'clock. It is now more than half-past. I request you to convey the remains to the grave at once.'

Tozer continued to read, ignoring him: 'And keep the charge of the Lord thy God, to walk in his ways, to keep his ...'

But Drury broke in again, and more indignantly: 'I have been waiting here over half an hour. Why can you not take the coffin to the grave and then come here and hold what service you please?'

Still managing to control his feelings, Tozer went on reading: '... to keep his statutes, and his commandments, and his judgments, and his testimonies, as it is written ...'

The others, however, though standing with bowed heads, were becoming restive, and when Drury, almost immediately, interrupted again – 'Again, I ask you to defer this service until after the remains have been interred.' – Gooding, Ramsey's employer, could stand it no longer.

'Pray, sir, *do* be quiet. The service will not last many minutes.'

'Don't tell me to be quiet!' cried Drury. 'I have a duty to perform and I shall do it. I must teach my parishioners that these proceedings are wrong.'

At that, Tozer closed his Bible and turned to Drury. 'I do not wish to offend your religious convictions or your conscientious scruples, but do let me beg of you to be quiet for a few moments. We shall not be long.'

'What has that got to do with it?'

'To *do* with it? I supposed you were a gentleman! A Christian! A minister of Christ!'

'I don't see what religious convictions or scruples have to do with it.'

'I do not want a discussion with you. I appeal to your manhood; I beg you not to torture the feelings of these poor people at a time like this.'

'Nonsense. Manhood? Feelings? What have they to do with it? Your proceedings are wrong, and I cannot and will not sanction them.'

'You have a priestly garb, but you are destitute of the spirit of your Master. I had thought if no Christian you might possibly be a man! But you have no spark of humanity or you would not be capable of this conduct.'

'I suppose you call that Christian!' said Drury, pointing dogmatically at the coffin with his umbrella. 'That child has not been baptized and is not a Christian, and I object to its being buried as such.'

Tozer lifted his fist in anger. 'If it were not for the feelings of these poor people, I'd soon silence your speech. You're a ... a disgrace to humanity!'

'Don't shake your fist in my face!'

'I was not shaking my fist in your face, but by God, you justly deserve to feel it!'

'And you call that Christian?'

'Perfectly. If this were not a funeral, I'd bundle you out of this meadow.'

Ramsey, the dead boy's father, then took a step towards Drury. 'Come, Mr Drury, I sh'll have somethin' to say if you don't allow this gentleman to go on with the service.'

And Sarah Ramsey, too, murmured to Tozer: 'Never mind the Parson, Mr Tozer, go on with the service.'

But Drury remained adamant: 'If you do not all at once take the remains to the grave, I shall lock that gate and go.'

'No one asked you to come,' said Tozer, 'and no one wishes you to stay.'

'I shall certainly lock that gate and leave if you do not remove the body at once!'

'Go to H ... Heaven if you like! It would be a deliverance if you and all your priestly tribe were there, but I fear you have a poor chance of getting there. Take yourself off. It is of no consequence to us where you go.'

As good as his word, Drury promptly locked the gate and stalked off along the footpath to Claydon, the eyes of the mourners angrily following him, and it was with some difficulty that Tozer brought the short service to a dignified conclusion. 'Friends ... Hard though it is, let us try to put this unpardonable interruption out of our minds, and give our thoughts to the body of Joseph Ramsey here before us, and hear, with reverence, the wisdom and consolation of these words of God.'

He then finished his reading: 'Behold, I show you a mystery; we shall not all sleep, but we shall all be changed. In a moment, in the twinkling of an eye, at the last trump ... So – when this corruptible shall have put on incorruption, and this mortal shall have put on immortality, then shall be brought to pass the saying that is written: Death is swallowed up in victory ... O death, where is thy sting? O grave, where is thy victory? ... Amen.'

The little party then broke up, some carrying and following the coffin round the side of the churchyard, some breaking through the hedge to find a way for it. Ultimately, it was lifted over the hedge and taken round to the north end of the churchyard, where the grave was ready. And that was how two-year-old Joseph Ramsey was buried – at the heart of a fight between clergymen. As the sexton put it, 'like a dog'.

This report of the incident, however, was published by the *East Anglian Daily Times*, and no-one knew who had written it. No reporters of other newspapers had been asked to attend, and why *should* they have been interested in the funeral of the unknown child of an unknown labourer? Immediately, there was a hard rejoinder from the *Ipswich Journal*, challenging the authenticity and objectivity of the report and defending Drury's action. Within two weeks, the story had spread like wildfire throughout the country. It was a national scandal. Letters to the press flocked in, with titles such as THIS INDECENT BRAWL; BOSH AND BUNKUM; A PESTILENT PRIEST; VILE, MONSTROUS LAW, and signatures like 'Full and Free Liberty', 'A Disgusted Layman' and 'One of the Haters of Humbug'. The seriousness of the controversy is reflected in this one extract:

Another generation will hear with wonder and with indignation of the law which now, in rural England especially, insults dissenters and all the unbaptised dead ...
With still greater surprise and shame will the clergy of that generation remember that it was the wearers of their cloth who clung to an inhuman and unchristian law when all other classes were anxious to remove it.

Some of the papers, such as the *Ipswich Journal*, went so far as to claim that the entire funeral, and its press publicity, was a deliberate political plot! But what could this mean? Why such a national uproar about this small incident, distasteful though it was, in this Suffolk meadow? Why was two-year-old Joseph suddenly national news?

A few things have to be remembered. This was 1878: just over 100 years ago. The population of England – of the living, and therefore also of the dead – had grown enormously with the Industrial Revolution. It had grown fourfold since the turn of the century. But almost all the burial grounds in the country belonged to the Church of England, and the growing population of the dead had nowhere else to go. Every man had the right, according to civil law, to be buried in his own parish churchyard, but ecclesiastical law said that only Church of England clergy could officiate, and that they should *not* read a Christian service over the bodies of the unbaptized. An intense conflict was therefore growing throughout

THE AKENHAM BURIAL SCANDAL.

In order that correspondents may clearly comprehend the facts of the case, we may point out that the service held by Mr. Tozer, which Mr. Drury interrupted, took place entirely outside the churchyard, and not in a corner of it, as some of our correspondents appear to imagine. We thought our report was clear upon this point, but repeat the facts in order that no mistake may occur.

To the Editor.

SIR,—I am ashamed to find that there can be found anybody to defend Mr. Drury's conduct. I know well

Yours, &c.,
FULL AND FREE LIBERTY.

the country and, at that very time, a Burial Law Reform Bill – one of many – was before Parliament. These are just a few examples of the heated speeches being delivered in the House of Commons. First, from a Member in Wales (John Bright):

I need not remind the House that this much aggravated problem is not confined to England. The majority of the people of Wales are Nonconformists. But in 1,426 out of 1,979 cases, no burial grounds at all are attached to the dissenting chapels in Wales. Why, even at the funeral of the Rev Henry Rees, the father-in-law of the Hon Member for Anglesey, nearly 1,000 people travelled from Liverpool, a distance of 80 miles, to attend the funeral of their Pastor, and yet were not allowed to hear a word spoken in the churchyard by any of the well-known ministers who were present! The situation and the law debars Nonconformist ministers from saying a word of comfort or exhortation to their own people at the graveside of their departed friends. Those who know the condition of Wales will readily understand that the Welsh are very anxious to have this grievance removed.

One English MP (H. H. Fowler) had an even wider foreign experience!

I am ashamed of being told, when I am in Austria, or Russia, or even Turkey, that England on this question is lagging behind the most bigoted countries in Europe. Why, Cyprus is miles ahead of us in the matter. The other day, an English soldier was buried in a Greek churchyard in Cyprus. Now if a Greek sailor had happened to die in a rural parish in England, he could only be buried by an Anglican clergyman with the rites of the Anglican Church. But what took place in Cyprus? Why, the burial service of the English Church was conducted by an English Chaplain. A Greek Priest was present, but the only part he took was to bless the grave! That poor Greek Priest might have taught a lesson of Christian charity to many an Anglican Bishop!

But other Members (for example, Mr Newdegate) were just as passionate in their defence of the existing situation – and for one central reason:

But Mr Speaker, Sir, I ask the Members of the House to remember that the proof of continuous identity in doctrine and services is essential to the validity of the title to all religious and denominational *property*! This Bill, by introducing the diverse services of different denominations into the churchyards of the Church of England will fundamentally invalidate our title to that property. The Church of England, in this respect, will be placed in a position of inferiority compared with every other denomination in this country!

Property! That was what was worrying the Church of England. A national problem and a national struggle was afoot. Could it be, then, that the Rev. George Drury was, after all, being made a scapegoat?

It turned out that the so-called newspaper report had, in fact, been written by none other than the Rev. Wickham Tozer himself. He had been persuaded to do so by Gooding and Smith – who were Dissenters, who were related to each other, and who were also related to a Mr Clarke who edited *The Christian World* and was ready to give the story immediate national exposure. Tozer was also encouraged, and assisted, by Frederick Wilson, the editor of the *East Anglian Daily Times*. Could it be, then, that this tiny scene in Suffolk was, in fact, a plot? Well, if it was, and the plotters had wanted to make the most of national sensationalism, they could not have picked a better man out of the whole country than the Reverend Drury. Firm Father George was the last man in England to take criticism lying down. He loved nothing more than a fight in the courts. He took the war into the enemies' camp, and sued the editor of the *East Anglian Daily Times* for libel. Soon the public were entertained by another outburst of colourful newspaper reports.

What sort of a man was Drury – who was ready to press religious disputation to extremes over the body of a two-year-old child under the very eyes of his mourning parents? Well, this is what he was like in the witness box; and these are just a few of the skeletons that were there to be drawn out of his cupboard. Mr Serjeant Parry was a well-known advocate, very skilled at cross-examination:

'I think you sometimes use very strong language to your opponents, do you not?'
'I think I do. I am rather a warm temper.'
'Do you know an association called the Church Association?'
'I know the Church Association.'
'Have you spoken of them as a body of assassins?'
'A body of what?'
'Assassins.'
'I have compared them to the Ancient Order of Assassins (laughter) but I have said that they were worse then the Assassins (renewed laughter). The Assassins acted openly!'
'Have you spoken of Protestantism, as it is called, as "poison"?'
'Very likely.'

* * *

'To come to the churchwarden and the state of the church. Did you know that Mr Smith of Rise Hall was churchwarden of Akenham?'
'I do not know whether he is churchwarden or not. My consent was never asked.'
'Do you mean to tell the jury you did not know that Mr Smith was the churchwarden of Akenham parish?'
'I do not know that he is.'
'Do you remember the Bishop and Rural Dean visiting Akenham Church in 1877?'
'Yes.'

'Was Mr Smith there as churchwarden?'

'Mr Smith was there.'

'As churchwarden?'

'Mr Smith was there.'

'What position was he in?'

'He was there.' (laughter)

'Was he treated by the Bishop and Rural Dean as the churchwarden of the parish?'

'I do not know that he was.'

* * *

'There is also an allegation in this article that you were under an admonition from your Bishop for lawless proceedings in your own church. Is that so?'

'No.'

'Do you know a Mr Steward?'

'Yes.'

'Did he, in May 1878 or thereabouts, come to you and serve you with a monition?'

'Mr Steward came to me in a meadow and informed me that he had a letter for me from the Bishop of Norwich, and I refused to receive it through him and I walked away.'

'Mr Steward is *here*: did he say it was a monition, or simply a letter?'

'He said a letter.'

'Did you say: "I only receive these things through the post"? Did Mr Steward thrust the document into your girdle which you then wore?'

'He did not, but he touched me with his hand.'

'Did you square up to him to fight him? Did you double your fist at him?'

'I think I did.'

'Did you call him a rascal?'

'No, I did not.'

'That you swear?'

'Yes.'

'Did you not take that paper that was in your girdle and throw it away?'

'I did not.'

'You complain in this court that your character as a priest of the Church of England has been attacked, and so on, but you have been under a monition more than once from your Bishop, have you not?'

'I have never received a monition from the Bishop unless that was a monition.'

Mr Steward's evidence, however, supported by that of the Bishop of Norwich, was rather different:

'You are Charles Richard Steward, a solicitor and registrar in Ipswich?'

'I am.'

'You have heard the Bishop of Norwich confirm that the Reverend Drury was under a monition from him; you have seen the judicial document produced in this court ordering the removal of certain articles and ornaments from the church; you have also heard that he recognized Mr Smith of Rise Hall as churchwarden and that he had directed that Mr Smith should have the keys of the church whenever he needed them ... and you have heard Mr Drury deny *all* these things. *Now*, would you tell us in your own words how you served the Bishop's monition in May of this year.'

'On Thursday, May 13th, 1878, I met the Rev. George Drury in a field in Claydon and handed him a duplicate of the monition. He refused to accept it, stating that he never received anything of the sort excepting through the post office. I told him it was my duty to deliver it to him in person, and on my attempting to place it within the girdle which he wore round his waist, he came at me with both his fists, and threatened to knock me down *totidem verbis* (laughter). I beckoned him away and requested him to act as one gentleman towards another. He replied that I was not a gentleman, but a rascal (laughter). He passed on and I told him I had served him personally, but he said I had not. I told him I should leave the document, together with the letter from the bishop, on the ground, which I accordingly did, then and there.'

The Bishop of Norwich also said that other proceedings had been taken against Drury some 14 years ago, and one or two of these were colourful, to say the least. One was about a nunnery in his village which Firm Father George supported:

'Now, about this question of the nunnery ... Upon one occasion, did you detain a young girl, about 16 years of age, in this nunnery against the will and the wish of her father?'

'Certainly not. A Miss Rolfe was admitted into our convent, but she was 21 years of age.'

'Did not the father of that young lady come to the nunnery and request that she should be given up to him?'

'I believe so, but I did not see him.'

'Did he not claim her, and did you not resist the claim by force?'

'He did not claim her of me at all. Some people broke into the convent. One of the persons who broke in, named Lovely, said to me: "Where is she?"'

'Did you resist the persons taking her away?'

'Yes.'

'Did you pour boiling water upon them?'

'No.'

'My question is: whether this lady was not in the nunnery; whether she was asked for by her father; and whether her being given up was not resisted by you, amongst others?'

'I will answer you in six words if you will allow me. Some labouring men and others were coming to break into our convent and take Miss Rolfe away. When these persons came I was sitting in the common room and heard a great noise at the back of the house. There I went and saw William Lovely, very active in breaking through the kitchen window. I threw a basin of cold water in his face and he ran away. After that they renewed the attack with large sledge-hammers on the doors and windows. When Lovely came up, he took hold of me by the coat collar, and another man – a blacksmith – by the arm, and they pulled me away ...'

'Was all this about the nunnery well-known in the county of Norfolk and the county of Suffolk?'

'Well known? Why, the newspapers and farmers have been going on in this way against me for more than 20 years. This libel that you are trying now is only a specimen of what they have been doing for more than 20 years!'

There was also another startling case:

'Now I ask you, were you ever fined for or charged with assault before the magistrates for striking one of your parishioners with a red-hot poker?'

'No. There you have gone too far. There was no red-hot poker in the case. I never assaulted the man at all.'

'Were you fined £5 for assaulting a parishioner in your church?'

'I was.'

'You say the red-hot poker is altogether a mistake of mine?'

'There was no poker in the case at all.'

'Was anything taken out of the fire by you, with which you struck the parishioner?'

'A piece of wire – for scratching out the stove.'

'A piece of wire? Not a poker? I have gone too far? How big was this piece of wire, then? And how long?'

'Well, about half an inch thick (laughter) and about, well, eighteen inches long, perhaps.'

Firm Father George clearly had his own definitions of pokers and pieces of wire! But still, to be fair, none of this behaviour was strictly relevant to the case in point. Some questions of truth, however, were. This evidence, for example, was clear enough. Drury had said quite emphatically: 'I did *not* receive any message that the burial could not take place until half-past five o'clock. I am perfectly *certain* that no message was left at my house.'

The employer, Gooding, however, swore that he had sent a young boy, William Fayres, to deliver the message: 'It was fixed at half-past five instead of five, because Mr Tozer could not get there as early as five as he had some engagement. I told Ramsey what I had done with reference to Mr Tozer, and I sent a boy named Fayres to Mr Drury to inform him of the postponement of the hour . . .'

William Fayres confirmed in court how he had done so: 'I was to say: "Please, Mr Drury, the funeral is to take place at half-past five in the afternoon", but if they could not be there quite at the time he was to forgive them, for they had to go a long distance. I took the message to Mr Drury's house. I saw an old lady and gave her the message. She said: "Stop a minute and then I will hear if there be any message back." She was away about one minute. I heard someone speaking. Then she came back and said: "There is no message back." I said: "Thank you"' (laughter).

So much for the evidence in court. Each in his own expert way, the advocates gave their summing-up. On some counts Drury's evidence was certainly less than convincing. Whatever the rights and wrongs of the ecclesiastical and theological issues involved – and whatever the striking nature of Drury's character – on some matters he seemed by no means concerned to stick close to the truth. But what was the result? The judgment went in his favour; according to the letter of the law he had been libelled. But that was not the whole judgment. Drury had claimed £2,000 damages – the judge awarded him 40 shillings. It was a legal victory, but a moral defeat. And two more things happened.

First, money poured in from all over the country to meet the costs of the editor of the *East Anglian Daily Times* – from people signing themselves 'Half-Inch Wire', 'Father, Mother and Five Little Heathens', and so on. In fact, more money was subscribed than was needed, and the editor, Frederick Wilson, used some of it to erect a small headstone for Joseph Ramsey. Secondly, in 1880 the Burial Law Reform Act was passed. The great world entered into the events that took place in this small Suffolk meadow, and what took place here affected the great world. The Akenham Burial Case changed the law of the land.

It seemed like the end of the story; but not for Mr Joseph Thurston, keeping his close eye on the affairs of the world through the newspapers in his home at 42, The Buttermarket. In 1895 – 16 years later – he noticed another article, and pasted another cutting into his book.

The remains of the late Rev George Drury, rector of Claydon and Akenham, were committed to the grave on Saturday afternoon ... The coffin, covered with lovely wreaths of flowers, was carried upon a bier, the bearers wearing blue cassocks and white surplices. With the clergy were the choir, at whose head was a cross-bearer, and who wore scarlet cassocks and white surplices. Candles were lighted in the somewhat gloomy interior, and during the service the odour of incense could be distinguished.

As the body, the mourners and congregation left the church the grand *Dead March* in *Saul* was played upon the organ. The family vault in the churchyard had been opened and in it the body was deposited. At the end of the service, the hymn 'On the Resurrection Morning' was sung ... The body was enclosed in an elm shell and a massive oak coffin lined with lead, with brass fittings. The inscription on the coffin plate was:

GEORGE DRURY
Born March 2nd, 1819
Died December 2nd, 1895.
R I P

A dramatic ending to Joseph Thurston's story!

But I was also interested in the other funeral that had taken place a long time before. What had finally happened to the two-year-old boy who, without knowing it, had been at the heart of this nation-wide scandal? When I first found Joseph Thurston's story, and drove over to Akenham, I had no idea what I would find. A hundred years seems a long time. I did not know that Drury's rectory would still be there, and his family vault – under a yew tree and overgrown with nettles and elder, edged with the words *'Domine Miserere'*. I did not know that the nunnery would still be there with its old chapel beams and stained-glass windows, its small room for 'Silence', and the back-kitchen grate and window where Drury threw his bowl of water (hot or cold?) over Lovely's head.

When I found Akenham Church, I made my way round to the north end of the churchyard. The ground was all overgrown with coarse grass, and there was only one stone leaning over in one corner. I went across to it, not expecting to find anything, but it was, in fact, the very stone I was looking for:

> 'Suffer little children – Forbid them not to come unto me,
> For of such is the Kingdom of Heaven.'

Akenham Church is closed now – a relic of earlier times – but, in my opinion, this small stone should be regarded as nothing less than a national monument.

As I said at the beginning, it all seemed to happen by accident. But then ... I wonder? Was Joseph Thurston's diligent keeping of all these newspaper cuttings, over so many years, in his quiet rooms in The Buttermarket, an accident? Was Mr Wilson's decision to publish and be damned – to uphold the freedom, the professional standing, the responsibility of the press through the courts; to take a definite stand on an important political issue – an accident? Was his decision to erect Joseph Ramsey's headstone at the north end of Akenham churchyard – the only stone that remains – an accident? Was my own searching for such stories of human significance – now in danger of being lost among the dusty piles on East Anglian floors and shelves – an accident? Well, call these things what you like; there were certainly strange chains of events here, in a story that reappeared and almost told itself in such a timely fashion.

A Postscript

That, too, would be a pleasing and satisfying end to my own story. But such stories do not end; one's judgment about them is never finally settled; and they and the people who were involved in them are more deeply written into our present-day society and, perhaps, exercise a much wider influence than we may realize.

Since I discovered this story, the living descendants (grandchildren) of most of those who took part in it have been in touch with me. The Drurys – from Australia and Japan; the latest Wickham Tozer (Mr Wickham Partridge, a Suffolk county councillor) from Long Melford; Rachel Smith – descendant of the Goodings at Akenham – from near Felixstowe; Joseph Thurston's grand-daughter from near Leicester; and even the descendants of Edward and Sarah Ramsey from Ipswich – all have written and have had much to add to the Akenham story. One thing that pleased me greatly was to have a characterization of the Ramseys, who seemed to figure only as characters of small significance in the national scandal as it developed, and who were dropped into the background as 'mere labourers'.

Mr Edward Ramsey (a well-sinker) was a quiet, gracious gentleman, with deep Christian principles.
His wife was a devout woman of very strong character, and proud to fight for her religious convictions.
(A truly grand old lady in her poke-bonnet.)

All these people carry the memory of the affair into their lives now, and their own personalities have, to some extent, been influenced by their recollections of the stand taken in it by their forebears. But they have also thrown some new light on the influence of the scandal and on its chief characters – Drury, Wickham Tozer and Frederick Wilson.

As to the influence of the Akenham case, it was interesting to hear from a man in Jersey who had been doing some research on the burial grounds there. He wrote:

I found a great deal of information, including several references to the 1880 Act, which, until I heard of Akenham, were mostly unintelligible. For instance on the 16th July, 1880, the Rector of the Parish of Granville here drew the attention of the States, or local Parliament, to the passage of a bill through the English Parliament – the 'Burial Bill'. Before this, on 10th September 1879, one of the local Judges, who in those days sat in Parliament as well, asked for the reviewing of the local laws which obliged dissenters and others to be buried in certain other places in the Island, but he was referred to a Committee, which at the time I did not understand, but now I do. He was being 'stonewalled' as, obviously (I had not noticed the national news on the front page) the news of the row in England, sparked off in Akenham, spread.

To cut a long and interesting story short, the influence of the Akenham Burial Case went beyond even the Parliament and shores of Britain and had a significant effect on the law of the Channel Islands.

But most interesting of all was the new information that came in about Drury and Wickham Tozer. In the publicity surrounding the case, especially in the press treatment of it, there is no doubt that Drury came off worst. It was he who was made to appear the man most lacking in humanity – a man of fanaticism and unreason. Is this a fair judgment? Or was there more justice than, on the surface, there seemed to be in his own claim that the 'Protestants' of the local villages had been baiting him for decades? Certainly it is clear that Drury faced many difficulties as the one High Anglican in a community consisting almost wholly of East Anglian Dissenters. In their nostrils incense *was* poison; the robes of Church of England parsons *were* the indescribable petticoats of the Roman Catholic priests. 'Down with the Papists!' 'No Popery!' – gangs of labourers were always chanting these slogans, and stoning the rectory. Drury had to build a nine-foot wall round his rectory to protect it.

But what a graceful and comfortable home this gave the Drury family inside – and Father George loved his home. He had other sides to his nature; creative, artistic, domestic. He had a brick kiln in his garden and made his own bricks. He built high walls round a sheltered kitchen garden, and strange gazebos from which there were pleasant views. He built fashionable 'ruins'. And he was also a skilled amateur stone carver. The pulpit in the church is said to be his own work, and at the top of the church tower are figures of saints and beasts carved by him, though they are very worn now. In the gardens, too, is an underground grotto, rather like a Second World War air-raid shelter, completely lined with shells and flints, and made by Drury and his daughters. They went over to Aldeburgh by pony and trap to collect the shells from the beach there. None of these, it would seem, the activities of an ogre?

And there is another story. It is said that there was one occasion when the retired village schoolmaster could not find a house and was evicted. Standing with his furniture in the road, he was in despair until Drury came up to him and said: 'One of my glebe houses is empty, you may have it.'

'After all my spiteful treatment of him,' said the schoolmaster, always a virulent opponent, 'Mr Drury is the only real gentleman in the village.'

This, however, is only hearsay. But what is not hearsay is another case in the courts when Drury, together with others, was facing an action by Father Ignatius, the famous 'monk' (and founder of Llanthony Abbey in Wales) whom Drury had, in early times, supported. In this case, which was over an ecclesiastical property, there is no doubt that it was Drury who showed reason and tolerance, and also a readiness to go to considerable personal (financial) expense to re-introduce into the Church of England those elements of religious life – such as the Monastic Orders – in whose truth and value he believed. There were certainly dimensions in Firm Father George which the Akenham Burial Case did not reveal. Is it possible then that, despite the powerful public image left by the press reports and the court case, Drury was misrepresented? Was there, despite all the appearances, something of a plot?

The evidence as to the actions of Wickham Tozer and Frederick Wilson demonstrates, without question, that they *did* know what they were up to, at least when they decided to confront Drury in the courts. It is perfectly clear, from this first letter from Frederick Wilson to Tozer, after the publication of the first newspaper report, that Tozer had written his initial article with the deliberate intention of pressing the cause of Burial Reform.

THE EAST ANGLIAN DAILY TIMES

Ipswich Aug 27, 1878.

Dear Sir,

The wide-spread commendation which your "graphic" report has already received must be sufficient assurance to you of the admirable manner in which it was done. Permit us to add our own special thanks and compliments. You have undoubtedly given an immense impetus to the cause of Burial Reform.

Yours sincerely

Fred W Wilson

Rev Wickham Tozer
Ipswich

And when Drury's libel action was threatened, the following sequence of Wilson's letters (to Tozer, who was then in Liverpool) makes their actions and intentions very plain.

THE DAILY TIMES IPSWICH

Oct 14, 1878.

Dear Sir,

I am threatened with an action for the "malicious and libellous report" of the Akenham Burial Case published in the "East Anglian Daily Times". I think that Mr Drury ought to be gratified but do not think that the East Anglian Daily Times should bear the whole brunt of the battle. Such an action by

THE EAST ANGLIAN DAILY TIMES.

EVERY MORNING. ONE PENNY.

The only Daily Paper printed in SUFFOLK, ESSEX, or CAMBRIDGESHIRE
Circulates extensively amongst the Nobility, Gentry, Clergy, and the Legal, Agricultural,
Shipping, and Commercial Classes

Ipswich, *Aug 27* 1878

Dear Sir,

The wide-spread commendation
which your "Graphic" report has
already received must be
sufficient assurance to you
of the admirable manner in
which it was done. Permit
us to add our own special
thanks & compliments. You
have undoubtedly given an
immense impetus to the cause
of Burial Reform.

Yours sincerely

Revᵈ. M. Wilson

Revᵈ. Wickham Tozer.
Ipswich

Mr Drury would do more to further the Burials Bill than any step I can imagine, and I trust the friends of Religious Liberty, now so thick around you, will come forward to help us. I want to form a guarantee fund of £500 to defend this action, and if he brings it, to attack him simultaneously under the Public Worship Act. You are aware that Mr Drury has already been admonished by the Bishop, and three parishioners (one of them his own Churchwarden) are ready to take action. I want you to set to work and get £200 guaranteed in the North, more if you are able. If there is any bottom in this talk about the Burials Bill there should be no difficulty in getting plenty of money to fight such a cause.

Hoping to hear that you are successful as you ought to be,

> I remain
> Yours truly
> *Fred W Wilson*

Rev Wickham Tozer

THE DAILY TIMES   IPSWICH

Oct 14, 1878.

Dear Sir,

I have written the enclosed as a letter for you to show in case of need. Drury's action is entirely founded on the report which he declares to be untruthful, malicious, and everything else that's bad. His present intention is no doubt to fight but I fear he will back out if he sees we are ready. To do that I must get this guarantee fund as I cannot fight this public question alone. Of course the money though guaranteed may never be required, or only part of it. We must be able to put Drury in the witness box and let him stand the fire of a good cross-examiner. I know I can rely on you to do *your* best and you are in the very place to succeed.

I shall be thoroughly ashamed of this talk about the Burial Bill if you have any difficulty in getting £200 or £250 guaranteed.

I send you a few copies of the paper containing the report – we have but very few copies left.

I have written to Mr Clarke of the "Christian World" asking him to join, and have already obtained one £50 guarantee in the neighbourhood.

I have no doubt we can get more and the cream of Liberalism in the country, now assembled in Liverpool, will doubtless come out more and strike a telling blow against clerical intolerance.

> Yours faithfully,
> *F W Wilson*
> per T R Eckington
> Excuse Mr Wilson not
> signing, he left the office
> before letter was ready
> for signature.
> *T R E*

Rev W Tozer.

Ipswich Oct 15th, 1878.

Dear Sir,

I have received your telegram and intend to go to London tomorrow to see Mr Clarke, of the "Christian World", who has taken the matter up warmly. You must set to work in Liverpool and get us all the support you can in the shape of guarantees to a Defence Fund. If I fight the matter it will be entirely on public grounds. Of course I could get out in a minute by giving up the name of the author of the report but that is very far from my desire. We must work the matter together and evoke all the enthusiasm and downright help we can from the friends of Religious Liberty – fight and beat him.

Relying upon you for your share,

> I remain
> Yours truly
> *Fred W Wilson*

p.s.

Telegraph to me tomorrow to Christian World office as to what you can do in the North.

This plan of action also clearly involved Clarke, the editor of *The Christian World*.

It is too much, then, to say that the actual burial of Joseph Ramsey was itself a plot, but it is not too much to say that, once the incident had occurred, it was used and publicized to maximum effect by Gooding, Smith, Wickham Tozer and Frederick Wilson alike. And certainly the libel case was entered into with the deliberate design of exposing, and making publicity capital out of, the very vulnerable idiosyncrasies of Drury's nature and of his past circumstances, with the case for Burial Reform clearly in mind.

But Wickham Tozer was, too, a man of strong character, devoted to furthering humane ends and the public good. He was an ardent supporter of the Free Library in Ipswich and its chairman for many years. He was approached by many, including John Gorst, for help and advice on research into education. And, perhaps more notable than all his other activities, he was the first to conceive and establish a 'Labour Bureau' (later to be called Labour Exchanges) in East Anglia. Facing much hostility in this, he wrote:

In 1882–5, Ipswich, like many other places, was suffering from depression of trade. Hundreds of men, through want of employment, were destitute, and for two years I had the painful pleasure of saving them and their families from starvation, by giving them provisions twice a week, for four months in each year. Often as many as 500 were relieved in one week. Sick and weary of the work, and seeing there was no finality to it, I determined to devise some means of helping the men to help themselves, and render charity unnecessary. At that period Labour Bureaux were unknown. I had no example to follow and was, therefore, obliged to plan and start one without assistance from anyone except friends who supplied the money. Our aim from the beginning has been to prevent a congestion of labour by removing it from where it is *not* to where it is in demand; in this we have been entirely successful.

In the Akenham Burial Case, it is clear that a number of men of strong and worthy character – each committed to beliefs and principles in their own way – were thrown together by similar conditions, social changes and anomalies in the law, which inevitably had to be solved. And one moral that seems to emerge is that, in history, the more detail one knows, the harder it is to judge – or, at any rate, to be confident that one's judgment is sound.

5 The Call of Providence

But knowledge to their eyes her ample page
    Rich with the spoils of time did ne'er unroll;
Chill penury repress'd their noble rage,
    And froze the genial current of the soul.

Full many a gem of purest ray serene
    The dark unfathom'd caves of ocean bear:
Full many a flower is born to blush unseen,
    And waste its sweetness on the desert air.

* * *

The applause of list'ning senates to command,
    The threats of pain and ruin to despise,
To scatter plenty o'er a smiling land,
    And read their history in a nation's eyes,

Their lot forbad ...

Or ... did their lot forbid?

One thing you can safely say about English country churchyards is that you never know what you are going to find. And there is a second fact on which, in East Anglia, you can completely rely: it is that one clergyman always leads to another! And certainly, if I may anticipate the following story just a little, there was nothing about the Rev. William Gordon which was going 'to blush unseen' or 'waste its sweetness on the desert air'. The 'Call of Providence' would see to that!

One day, I was following up some details of the Akenham Burial story. The Rev. Wickham Tozer had been minister of an 'independent' chapel in St Nicholas Street, and I wondered whether it might still have records of him. Many buildings, however, have since been converted into shops and stores, and this one proved hard to find, so I began systematically to visit all the 'independent' chapels in Ipswich, and this led me, one afternoon, into a quiet churchyard behind an old Congregational chapel now known as the Tacket Street Union Reformed Church. The graveyard was very small, almost of pocket handkerchief size, bounded by a low stone wall and black iron railings, and was beautifully kept, with grass regularly cut and rolled, as smooth as the lawns of a Cambridge college, and a variety of trees – ash, willow, cherry, laburnum, shiny-leaved holly trees and dark green yews. Above all, in the afternoon sunlight, it was peaceful. The caretaker was busying himself, in a pleasantly indolent fashion, with tidying up a rubbish heap and tending a bonfire which was smouldering nearby. The grey smoke curled, hovered, and puthered slowly up through the branches. It was a typical, placid, East Anglian afternoon.

The caretaker was young, friendly, rosy-cheeked, and very ready to help. So much so, that, the minute I approached him, we found ourselves talking at cross-purposes. The moment I said I was tracking down a clergyman, he grinned broadly, nodded and indicated a headstone beside the rubbish dump. An old yew tree had grown partly into the grave before growing straight up and spreading its branches over it.

'Oh, ah!' he said, 'I know him. Thar he is.'

But I was a bit bemused. The engraving said 'The Rev. William Gordon, D.D.' I shook my head. 'That's not him,' I said. 'The man I'm after was called Wickham Tozer.'

'Oh, ah?' he looked blank. 'Wickham Tozer? That don't sound right to me ... I tell y'what. You 'ad better come into the vestry, because all the pastors' pictures are up on the wall, and there are some notes on the Rev. Gordon.' So we went inside; into the vestry, to the pictures on the wall and the notes. And for a while, the Rev. Wickham Tozer and the Akenham Burial Case were completely forgotten.

From a print published in London in 1796, the face of William Gordon looked down at me, and, with even the little provisional knowledge contained in the notes, I went outside again to linger a little over the grave there; indeed, to marvel at it. For who do you think it was who was lying by the rubbish dump in this quiet corner of Ipswich? It was the man who had once been private secretary to George Washington – General George Washington, the first President of the United States. The man lying here, unknown and undisturbed for almost 200 years, had not only been alive at the time of the American Revolution – the War of Independence – and had not only witnessed it, but had actually taken part in it. The ears of the Rev. William Gordon, D.D., had once heard not only the sounds of the peaceful East Anglian countryside, but also the crack of American muskets and the bugles of the American Army.

Rev.ᵈ William Gordon D.D.

What is more, he was on their side! The British had put a price on his head. The man lying here was one of those many East Anglian Protestants, English Dissenters, who had been actively involved in the making of the United States – the New World – in the designing and hoisting of the Stars and Stripes.

I had to leave the Tacket Street churchyard then, but a little later I learned that other materials from Gordon's own hand were in the Ipswich archives: some detailed notes of a paper he had once delivered to a committee of the provisional Congress of Massachusetts and, much more interesting, a large number of letters he had written to his daughter, wife of an Ipswich draper. Gradually, William Gordon's story took shape.

Born at Hitchin, Hertfordshire, in 1728, he was ordained at Ipswich in 1754. The Tacket Street Church was founded in 1686 as an old meeting house, by a Rev. Langston (a Langston Hall in the chapel commemorates him), and Gordon initially joined this church to help a Rev. William Notcutt. Notcutt died in 1756 and Gordon took over. The first thing that becomes quite certain from that point on is that, at least during the time when he was Pastor in Ipswich, Gordon was no great shakes as a clergyman. The record says very simply:

When Mr Gordon took over as Co-Pastor, the membership was 17 men and 36 women, a total of 53 ... During his 8 years as *sole* pastor, there were only 5 admissions. This, indeed, was a poor period in the history of the church.

But a second thing is also certain. From that time on, William Gordon always kept his ears wide open for the 'Call of Providence'. Whenever it sounded, he followed; wherever it beckoned, he was ready to go. And it seemed to whisper to him a good deal during the years that followed. Indeed, there were many times when he seemed to anticipate it, prepare for it and help it along in suggesting what its directives should be. The next entry in the record is this (my italics):

The Rev W Gordon being invited to take upon him the pastoral charge of the Church of Christ late under the care of the Rev Dr Jennings of London deceasing, and *having sought direction from above and consulted friends, came to a conclusion to comply with what appeared to be the voice of providence*, and, on June 3rd, 1764, quitted the pastoral office and received his dismission in order to a removal.

May the blessing of God overrule the
said event for the general benefit of all
concerned.
        Amen.

The Church of Christ in London was at Gravel Lane, Wapping. William Gordon, at the age of 36, was on the move – but not only to Wapping! The Call of Providence had only just begun.

For the next five years, Gordon revelled in the life of eighteenth-century London. He preached far and wide – Ponder's End, Tooting, Hitchin, Biggleswade; and he sup't and dined far and wide – in The White Hart at Bishopsgate, The Angel in Whitechapel, Canonbury House in Islington, The Falcon at Gravesend. He bought books from Dilly's in The Poultry. He listened to the preaching of famous clergymen, such as Mr Whitefield.

And all the time, small legacies came his way, sometimes materializing even out of his troubles. He came to believe, for example, that he could not 'in conscience baptize children in the large way to which I had become accustomed', and decided not to baptize children unless, in at least one parent, there was 'real subjection to Jesus'. Finding this a difficult distinction to make, he ruled that he would not baptize a child unless at least one of its parents was a church member. This made him decidedly unpopular, and a majority of the church wanted a 'consultation against his continuance' – one of the most influential voices being that of a Mr Curtis, brother of 'one of the bigotted clergymen at Birmingham'. Gordon therefore 'defended his sentiments by preaching two discourses' and, lo and behold!

Mr Curtis said he had not thought I had so much to say for myself. When he died, within a year or two ... he left me a twenty pound legacy; which was altogether unexpected.

Also, one May, he visited Tunbridge Wells

to drink the waters in order to compose my mind and invigorate my body ... Whilst there, I studied a funeral sermon for Mrs Jennings, the widow of the Dr whom I succeeded,* and preached it in the afternoon of the 27th, in which I introduced something relative to our parting, and by which I meant to avoid the painfulness of a farewell discourse ... She left me a legacy of ten pound.

Legacies, obviously, were significant items in a pastor's income.

But Gordon experienced difficulties quite apart from those of a religious nature. One September (25th):

Removed to Lemon Street, Goodman's Fields. The King of errors having at the command of the King of Kings served an ejectment upon our landlady, so that our house upon Stepney Causey, with those of others, fell to a new possessor.

* i.e. the Rev. Dr Jennings.

Tacket Street meeting house in Gordon's day

The same were sold by auction. Many of the tenants purchased theirs; but mine falling to the lot of another person we were under the necessity of moving to a new habitation, not so pleasant as the former, but far better than we deserved.

Again, even in such an incident, William Gordon saw the hand of the King of Kings. Providence was still calling through the thick of circumstance and, indeed, was beginning to whisper from overseas – from America. During the 'baptism troubles', some members of his Wapping Church had even 'insinuated, from what favourable speeches had been made by me in behalf of America, that it was a scheme of mine – that so I might move thither.' How accurate their interpretation of his motives was, Gordon does not say, but what is certain is that throughout his experiences in London, he was continually going down to the quayside to say goodbye to friends who were setting off for America, and it is interesting to remember that by this time the seaway to the New World – from East Anglia to the West – was a regular thoroughfare. It was as long a period *before* Gordon was living in London as it has been from then to the present day that the first East Anglian Dissenters – part of the great movement of European Protestantism moving west – had sailed from England to make a New England. It was 140 years since John Winthrop had taken his fleet across the Atlantic, with a well worked-out plan of colonization, and now the avenues of sea-going trade, of commerce and finance, and even of insurance, were well established, as were large networks of personal acquaintance and influence.

Whatever the substance of his congregation's insinuations, and whatever the exact timing of the Call of Providence, on 25 May 1769, William Gordon saw a Mr Beatty and a Mr Hacket on board ship at Gravesend 'in order to return to America'. In June 1770, at his own desire, the following testimonial was drawn up:

At my desire the following was drawn up and wrote out fair upon parchment with the left hand of Mr Deeble.

This is to notify all whom it may concern, that the Reverend William Gordon successor to the late Reverend Dr Jennings, Pastor of a Church of Christ meeting in Old Gravel Lane Wapping, is an approved Minister of unexceptionable character, well known to, and heartily recommended by us, whose Names are hereunto subscribed.

London, June 1770.

*John Rogers
Thos Towle BD
*William Ford Jnr
John Stafford
*John Macgowan
*Joseph Pitts
William Clarke AM
Samuel Palmer
Rich Winter BD
Joseph Barber
Saml Brewer BD
Rice Harris DD
*Benj Wallis
*Patrick Ashworth DD
Sam Stennett DD
*Sam Morton Savage DD

*David Muir AM
*I Watson DD
Nath Jennings
John Trotter DD
Abrm Broth
William Smith AM
*Frans Spilsbury
*Jas Webb
*Edward Hitchin BD
Edward Venner
*John Olding
Andrew Kippes DD
Merdith Townsend
*Wm Porter
*Wm Langford DD
*Thomas Gibbons DD

*John Condor DD	*John Walker LLD
*Samuel Wilson	*Philip Furneaux DD
Abraham Rees	Thos Toller
I Thompson Jnr	*Hugh Farmer
*Edw Pickard	H Mayo Mot
*Geo Stephen Mot	Rich Amner (I think is dead)
*William Prior	

Mr Beatty's recommendation unknown to myself procured me from Princeton College the honour of Master of Arts in 1765; I kept it a profound secret from everyone, and it was not known by any of my brethren while I was in England.

The signatures on this testimonial are interesting in themselves. Was, for example, the Samuel Palmer here related to (son of?) or connected with the Samuel Palmer who exercised such an influence on Benjamin Franklin? But the most interesting part of this document, and the real reason why I include it, is the little paragraph at the end, which was originally written alongside the signatures on the left.

From the beginning, I had wondered about the origin of William Gordon's 'D.D.' – what might have been the source of his degree – and here was at least a beginning. Education was also well established in the New World! Not only the Call of Providence in 1769 and 1770, but also Mr Beatty and Princeton College had been active five years earlier. Of such stuff, too, it seems, is Providence made. And in 1770 a more influential person, with a more effective offer, entered the scene. This was none other than Benjamin Rush (later to be one of the signatories to the Declaration of Independence), who had just gone back to Philadelphia after pursuing his studies in Scotland and France. On 12th July, Gordon received a letter from the post office at Deal:

Its arrival was very providential, and at once fixt to what point of the compass we should direct our course, when crossing the Atlantic. It held forth a probability of settling at Philadelphia, but gave assurance of numerous vacancies, affording the prospect of great usefulness and comfort: and contained an invitation to his house, till we could get a settlement. The language was strong, pathetic, and animating.

The way was now open, and arrangements were put in hand:

The first business was to procure a passage in a suitable vessel. We heard of one that was to sail for Philadelphia the latter end of August, commanded by

* Sending this copy to his daughter much later, he marked with an asterisk all those ministers who had since died. He also wrote: 'Wilkes's *North Briton*, No 45, made such a noise about this time, that Mr Hitchin said he hoped the signing ministers would not be just 45, but so it happened, without any design.'

Capt Sparks. I employed my friend Mr John Thompson to examine the ship. She was about 250 tons burden, and was perfectly to his mind, so that he said he should desire no better to go round the world with. Capt Sparks agreed to take £50 for our and our maid's – Debby's – passage, and to carry our boxes and freight free.

All was ready – but here again, Providence, as we shall see, played a strange trick. On the point of sailing, Gordon was struck down by a high fever. He insisted on going, however, against everybody's advice, because everything was packed and on board ship. So a friend of his, Mr Keen, wrote secretly to George Whitefield, the famous preacher, who was then in Philadelphia, asking him to return Mrs Gordon and Debby safely to England because Gordon himself would most probably die on the passage. We shall see Providence's little quirk on all this later, after the Atlantic voyage, but another point is interesting here. All unknown to Mr Keen, William Gordon had not left such matters to chance. Like all good Dissenters, he had a business head on his shoulders, and had already taken his own precautions:

I had obtained a license from the London Annuity Society for going to live in any part of New England, New York, Jersey and Pennsylvania, and had insured my life on the voyage, for a sum, in case of death, that should equal the annuity in value.

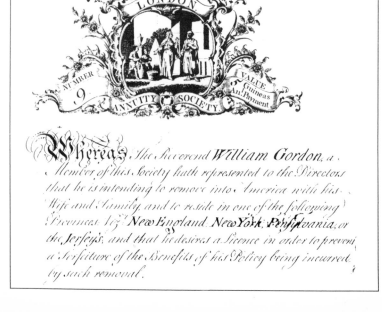

Later, this very insurance policy came to light and makes a most interesting document, but it carries another significance. If William Gordon was always ready to respond to the Call of Providence, he did so with something less than complete confidence in what it might entail. The King of Kings might call, but still ... it was just as well to have an insurance policy! This, as scholars like Max Weber have noted, was the way of European Protestants: faith – underpinned by works – and (just in case) financial profit and security.

Then – the Gordons were off, bound for the New World! It was soon clear that Providence had not the slightest intention that William Gordon should end his days on the Atlantic. On the contrary, the ocean enlivened him and 12 days out his fever was gone. He felt 'bravely' he said, and during the rest of the voyage he enjoyed every incident on board. He was continually enquiring, energetic, alive. One thing that was certain was that William Gordon was never going to miss anything that Providence put under his nose. Sometimes, he simply stood on deck at all times of day and night, wondering at everything he saw:

I was much entertained with the fiery sparks which were occasioned by the bows striking against the water and also by the sides of the ship. But though they had the appearance of fire, they had no heat in them and were luminous as it is thought by philosophers merely from fishy particles of matter akin to that shining substance which whitings and herrings possess ...

The night was delightful. I stood upon the deck late. How entertaining to sail steadily along, to observe the shining sea, to behold the bright moon, and to contemplate the distant stars.

Sometimes he watched flying fish chased by dolphins, and he had a go at fishing himself. This was how he described it to his daughter:

One such dolphin was captured by your parental friend. He got up early in the morning, secured a line and bait, went to the stern and cast out the snare. Here he sat patiently watching till the fish snapt and hung itself. He did not attempt pulling it in immediately for fear of losing it, but played with it till its strength was weakened, and observed that one while it appeared brown and at another time yellow, but whether these changes of colour were owing to anger, fear, to despondency or to bodily anguish, he was not philosopher enough to determine. When he thought he could get it on board safely, he pulled it up and having secured it, notified the capture – for he would not venture to boast before the deed was finished, lest he should feel silly afterward.

He noticed, too, how glad ships' companies were to meet with each other in mid-ocean, taking care to check their navigational calculations with each other. He himself even helped on the lookout.

About this time we were looking for the Gulf Stream which runs through the straits of Bahama along the Florida coast and so for many hundreds of miles northwards ... When, as we sailed westwards, we discovered sticks, grass, moss, etc. flowing northwards we were much gratified, as we knew we were nearing the American coast ... We also saw what the sailors called a Booby Bird, of the duck kind, belonging most likely to the Bermuda Islands which lie 500 miles east of Carolina. It was an acceptable sight as it tended to prove we were approaching land.

But when they got near the coast, a violent storm blew them off course. There was a squally, blowy night with heavy rain, roaring wind, cracking sails. The dead lights – large wooden frames – were fastened outside the cabin windows, and the passengers lighted oil lamps and were glad to keep to their state rooms and night berths; but not William Gordon:

I was desirous of gratifying my eyes with a sight of the sea in the tumultuous state of a violent storm, and accordingly crawled up on all fours, taking care to hold fast ... The whole sea had the appearance of a light whitish flame, but it appeared so in the strongest degree at the foaming tops of the head of the waves ... The captain said he scarce ever saw a worse night.

And after his sea adventure of two months, it was William Gordon who was the first to leap ashore in America – at Wilmington, only 30 miles from Philadelphia – not at all dead from fever, but very much alive.

We quitted the boat, and got up the side of a vessel laying close in with the wharf. When upon its deck the cap't congratulated me upon my safe *landing* in America, I perceived his mistake, stept forward, got first on shore, and upon *his* landing congratulated *him*. We went to the Royal George and there breakfasted. I also purchased cream, butter, apples and bread, which were a great treat – and later, we feasted upon apple dumplings.

But it was here that the strange trick of Providence was revealed. William Gordon, who had started his voyage apparently at death's door, was now vigorously enjoying apple dumplings on the shore of America, and his record of that first breakfast continues like this:

upon taking up my first Newspaper, there read the just published account of ... the death of the Rev'd Mr Whitefield, to whose care and kindness Mr Keen (who also lay dead on Monday o'er night) had recommended Mrs G in case I should die, as he feared before I reach't America ... I minuted down in my pocket-book: 'May I be profited by his removal.'

When Dr Benjamin Rush took Gordon to his first church service in Philadelphia, the pulpit was draped with black – but not for him. Providence had not yet done with William Gordon. Indeed, it sent him, that same evening, a warning to follow in the footsteps of George Whitefield and to practise his method of preaching. It was an anonymous letter:

Rev'd Sir,

As a great deal of your future success in this country may depend on your preaching tomorrow, it may not be amiss to advise you to be very cautious both in the choice of your subject, and manner of delivery – the congregation you are to preach to are more than Calvinistic, fond of a very warm and zealous delivery, of the doctrines of free grace, salvation by faith alone, and the extraordinary effusions and operations of the Spirit; they like to hear much of conversion by the instantaneous and sovereign agency of the Holy Ghost, and to be threatened with the loud vociferations of hell-fire and damnation. It will be prudent in you to hear the sermon in the forenoon where you intend to preach in the afternoon, that you may have a specimen of American doctrine, and mode of delivery. If you are not strictly orthodox, be sure you avoid such subjects as the above, and rather dwell on some practical point, with a long application, and deliver it warmly.

Let your conversation on religious subjects be with reserve. It is more than probable that some will call on you next week, invite you to their houses and pretend extraordinary friendship, only with a view to know if you are an Arminian, or not of their way of thinking – Take care where you lodge, and particularly the members of the congregation where you are to preach tomorrow – Unbosom yourself to none, until you know them thoroughly – If you are not thus guarded, external show and hypocrisy will destroy you – You can as yet have no idea of the peculiar tenets of our country; wait therefore with cautious prudence and silently hear rather than be first to offer your sentiments –

This, sir, is intended in friendship to a stranger, peruse it in private, and if it may be of any service to you in a strange land, the author's end is answered, who sincerely wishes that God may direct you for the best.

ps. The party with whom that congregation is connected, are both very numerous and powerful here.

The voice of Providence came from many and strange directions, but in matters of caution like this William Gordon always had the good sense to observe it.

When he landed in Philadelphia with so much zest for living, it was with the same questing spirit that had quickened all those Protestants who had sailed the Atlantic, settled and established all the colonies of America before him. But, at that very time, they themselves were already in rebellious mood over the imposition of the new Stamp Act of 1765 which curtailed the earlier liberty they had enjoyed. Into this New World of experience, and into its increasing unrest, Gordon rode with his unquenchable liveliness and curiosity, travelling and preaching all over Virginia, New York, Massachusetts and Boston. Every day, every journey, was filled with new observations, new enjoyments:

At Springfield saw an orchard of peaches in bloom; it was sixty acres large, and all but a small nook planted with peaches.

Came to Fleming Town and dined at the sign of Pitt, the worthy parent of the present bottomless Pitt!

Had a bird in my hand, just shot, much like the English red linnet in size, colour and bill ... The body in general brown, the breast a pale red, which was rather deeper on the head above the upper bill. The head was not red all over, only some way above the bill. Birds much like the English Tom-tit seen here in great plenty.

For two nights it froze ... The cold was so intense at night to congeal Hollands gin, set in a cup. When I preached at Dorchester and administered the sacrament, the bread was frozen ... To keep out Jack Frost what we could – having been assured he was a most biting fellow, and would at times thrust his cold talons between a man and his wife while abed – we pasted paper over the windows where there was danger that he would enter upon the wings of the wind, and had a fire in our chamber that we might moderate his assaults by a warm reception. However, we found the assertion verified, and could track him by his icy footsteps upon the sheets within the space intervening between our heads! . . . Have observed that the thermometer has often fallen, and manifested therein by the spirit a *colder* air, a little *after* the fire has been lighted, which I impute to the circulation occasioned by the fire's drawing off the warmed air of the chamber, and letting in colder from without.

Remarked that a cock-chafer, brown beetle, May Fly, or Old Witch as you please, was dug out of the ground with the maggot. Thus you see that they have *old* witches in the United States the same as in Great Britain, and I am sure they have *young* ones, tormenting the other sex till they have made a prey of them. Remember – you are to read this on your wedding day.*

One night at Western we were forced out of our beds by a daring attack from a number of bugs – and were obliged to get up and drop ourselves to sleep as well as we could in the chairs. The daughter of one of our people, who lay at the further end of the same room, was so fatigued with journeying that she slept soundly, tho' attacked by a host of these blood suckers, but we thought it best to let her sleep on.

When I had got to that part of Lancaster called Choxet, where the council was to be held, I learnt that I was time enough to go to the top of Wachuset mountain in Princetown boundaries, which has been found to be 2989 feet above the level of the sea; and in a clear horizon may be seen at the distance of 67 miles. I have been told that when the weather and time of day suits, you may see from the top of it one or other of the weathercocks on the steeples at Boston, with your eyes. Boston however is but about 36 miles by the road. Having no one to accompany me I went alone; and almost shudder at the thought of my having been so venturesome. I procured a fresh horse, my own being sufficiently tired; and the journey being about four miles and back again. After

* Taken from Gordon's letters to his daughter, Mrs M. F. Conder.

having rode far up the hill, or rather mountain, and surmounted various difficulties, I dismounted some distance below the summit; fastened my horse to a bush; and then proceeded to the top, which was quite clear of trees, flat in general, and encumbered with very little brushwood. The prospect was extensive every way, but not as clear and bright as to set it off to the best advantage. When I had gratified my curiosity, I commenced my return. I had taken care to remark where I entered, lest I should get into a wrong track. I pursued what I thought to be the right; but there were so many deviations, and it was so long to my apprehension, increased by a degree of anxiety and the approaching evening, before I saw my horse, that the sight of him rejoiced me. We descended with safety . . .

Always the adventurer, always the observer, always the scientist! He recorded that he loved the taste of bear-meat just as much as he loathed the taste of Dutch sour milk and bread made from potatoes. He also recorded the nature of some important social institutions. Marriage, for example:

The government of Massachusetts empowers Justices of Peace and pastors of churches to marry: but the parties are to be regularly published in the towns where the intended bride and bridegroom live. The town clerk's certificate of their being duly published justifys the minister in executing the service to which he is empowered; but he is not to exercise it unless one of the parties is an inhabitant of the town where he ministers. The ring is not used, except by episcopal clergymen. They may marry any time of the day or in the evening; it is most commonly in or towards the evening. Many go to the minister's house to be married; but in general, excepting quite the lowest class, are married at their own, their parents', or friends'. The ministers are not tied to any form: each follows his own judgment and inclination. When I married, I generally mentioned that it was not as a minister of the Gospel, but as a servant of government: that it was a business of such importance as made prayer upon the occasion proper . . . The legal fee was no more than three shillings sterling; but the lowest class generally gave a dollar or 4/6, and others more, as they pleased, and according to circumstances and the generosity they possessed. The minister took care to notify in a proper manner to the town clerk the marriage, who was paid three halfpence or two pence for the entry in the parish book, by which register the validity of it could be proved when wanted. When persons had been published, they might decline marrying for months; but if they changed their minds and wanted to marry another person, it could not be done till a year after the publication.

Just as he had been in England – with an eye on his legacies – throughout his American experiences, always, everywhere, Gordon was careful in weighing up the money which preaching allotted him:

Observe that the several congregations during the singing before the close of worship have a collection in boxes or a kind of cap-bag at the end of a long stick for the convenience of putting it to the end of the seat and to every person without going into the pew. Halfpence are generally put in, but besides copper, silver is also put in when they happen to be well pleased with the preacher ... On the 5th April was paid £32.2.2½ in Philadelphia, being the amount of what had been collected ... Thus I received in all for my labours in the capital of Pennsylvania £57.10.0½ whereas my expenses were but £40.14.4.

A profit in Pennsylvania in the service of the Lord! But soon he was made an established minister at Jamaica Plain, Roxbury – one of the three churches in Boston – and it is interesting to see that when receiving his invitation to this opening, William Gordon was at once convinced that, in it, he heard the Call of Providence.

When all expectations of settling either at New York or Philadelphia were at an end, the invitation to Jamaica Plain arrived, without my having any ground to expect such a thing. I viewed it as a particular providence. I therefore determined when I found I was acceptable to hearken to it ... There were such concurring circumstances that in my judgment made up a *call of providence*, and against that I dared not go. Besides, the situation of the Plain pleased me.

And when describing and weighing up the details of the offer, he recorded the way in which the appointment of a minister took place:

When a parish is without a minister, they invite a person to preach as a candidate. After a while they call a parish meeting in the place of worship, the male inhabitants attend, and if the majority agree to give the candidate a call to be their minister, the majority of that church having agreed to choose him as their pastor, they propose to raise him a yearly salary, to furnish him with so much wood for firing, and to allow him so much money as a *settlement*, which is to assist in building or purchasing a house for himself, and which is to remain his property wholly and entirely, so that he can leave it or sell it. The parish when they give this settlement view their minister as tied down to them for life, and if he leaves them, when they would retain him, they consider themselves as entitled to a return of a part, according to the number of years he has been with them, whether less or more.

Once agreed, all these details became obligations in the law, and the third church and parish at Roxbury offered Gordon a salary of '£100 [American] per annum lawful (or £75 sterling) together with 21 cord of wood for firing' – and there was no need of a 'Settlement' because the parish owned a ministerial house of which he could have the use. But there was also another item:

It was further agreed that I should have for my own all the *unmarkt* money. Before the congregation is dismissed on the Sabbath, the deacons carry about the box to the several pews. Many pay the quota of their assessment towards the *expense* of supporting the minister *gradually*, by putting it into the box wrapt up in paper – from time to time more or less – with their name upon it. This *markt* money is credited to their account by the treasurer of the parish, though paid to the minister weekly, which supplies him with running cash. Strangers or non-parishioners, will put in the box *mere* money, which of course is *unmarkt*! This does, in some places and at certain times, prove *considerable*.

The Call of Providence was therefore 'hearkened to', and Gordon went to Boston. Before long he was an overseer at Cambridge College, chief clerk to the Ecclesiastical Council, and then – when, as he put it, 'the flame of liberty blazed out' – secretary to George Washington. His letters after that, during the War of Independence, read like something out of *Davy Crocket* or *The Last of the Mohicans*. If Mrs Gordon and Debby went with him, which they sometimes did, they would go by covered wagon. But Gordon himself always went by horseback, crossing rivers and lakes on flat-bottomed boats, and often with military escort.

We were joined by three American soldiers, who were to be the guide to our destination, and took provision for ourselves and horses. When we had travelled as we thought long enough, we stopt, one of the soldiers struck fire with his firelock, and lighted a small quantity of flax or hemp, which, being communicated to dry leaves and sticks, soon furnished us with a good fire. We eat and drank, rested and were refreshed, and then went on ... to Fort George to see a colonel who was ill, but I was against tarrying there, for I thought we might not be out of reach of hostile Indians.

One night, having crossed the Connecticut River, he and some civilian colleagues gave up their lodgings to a company of soldiers.

We were gentlemen commoners, whilst they were gentlemen soldiers in the American service, engaged on the side of liberty. We lay for the night in peastraw – quite dry. We did not strip, but went to bed with our clothes on. I was not very warm after burying myself on the best of my judgment, but upon the whole rested very well. In the morning discovered that one of my silver buckles had in some of my motions quitted my shoe, but, after feeling about for it a while, I recovered it.

He was as much on the watch for the hostile British as the hostile Indians! The men he dined and supt with were the officers of Washington's army: Washington himself; John Adams – who helped to draft the Declaration of Independence, and who was to be second President of the United States; Samuel Adams, who organized the destruction of the tea in Boston harbour; Hancock; and Governor Hutchinson – 'that firebrand', said Gordon, 'that afterward kindled the war between the mother country and the colonies'.

But if Gordon agreed in supporting the rebellion against the British Government, he also spoke out just as fearlessly before the General Court of Massachusetts when he thought their authority was being exercised in questionable ways.

We have, gentlemen, been and are still engaged in a glorious contest for securing our rights and privileges; begun at first in opposition to the arbitrary demands of a British parliament ... We have expended much treasure and sacrificed thousands of lives in resisting a foreign tyranny ... But to what end, should there rise up in our own borders a legislative power that shall claim and exercise the right of altering wills . . . to gratify the humours, or to serve the interests of a few individuals? Are we beggaring the country and shedding some of the best blood in it, only to transfer the tyranny of a British parliament to an American General Court?

This is forthright, rousing oratory, but it is no surprise to learn that the liberty Gordon was so stoutly defending was that of leaving property! His speech went on:

We mean to secure to ourselves and posterity all the valuable and imputed privileges of human nature; but how is this possible should any delegated body trample upon the rights and liberties of the living and the *dead*. I mention the right and liberties of the dead! ... Among these is that of lying in the place or vault they have made choice of while living, attended either by the bow and arrows, the tomahawk and scalping knife, the sword and buckler, or the gold and jewels and treasure which they directed should be deposited with them ... But much more is it deemed their right to have the *property* they lately possessed disposed of according to their last will and testament!

There were seven long, detailed and closely argued pages of Gordon's submission to the committee, and even he feared that he might have bored his listeners: 'If, Gentlemen,' he concluded, 'I have wearied your patience, I ask your forgiveness, and hope never to offend more in the same way.' No doubt they were aware that wills and legacies formed a subject close to Gordon's heart.

Gordon's letters to his daughter also contain one or two secrets which, to the best of my knowledge, history does not yet know. He believed, for example, that a collision between the British Crown and the American colonies could be avoided and was in communication with Lord Dartmouth, in England, through a Mr Thornton, and was quizzed about this on one occasion. No less a person than Samuel Adams and two 'patriotic delegates' came to breakfast with him 'to converse upon the American grievances'.

After a long conversation, I said 'Gentlemen, what will satisfy you?' Mr Samuel Adams answered 'Let the British Government set us down as we were in the beginning of '63, and that will content us, and this you may write to Lord Dartmouth.' I knew Mr Samuel Adams to be a thorough politician, and immediately concluded he designed to discover whether I corresponded with Lord Dartmouth. In order to lead him into the belief of the contrary, I directly answered 'I never received a line from Lord Dartmouth in my life' – which was true, literally, for though I wrote to him under server to Mr Thornton, he never sent me a line; but mentioned to Mr Thornton after he had read my letter what he thought, which, when it was intended, Mr Thornton communicated to me. When we had broke up, and Mr Samuel Adams was completely taken in, I took the first opportunities of writing to his Lordship under cover to Mr Thornton and of acquainting him with what would give full satisfaction to the colonies. Mr Thornton informed me in answer that his Lordship was fully determined, when an opportunity offered, to bring forward the repeal of the obnoxious acts.

Gordon was obviously at the heart of much political and military intrigue:

Sup't at Capt. Heath's, later a General in the American army. Somebody proposed to him that as affairs were extremely critical, and as governmental despatches came from England to General Gage by way of New York, he should go to New York, wait the arrival of the packet, and watch his opportunity of stopping the Postman between that and Boston: then take out what was intended for Gage; by which means the Sons of Liberty might gain important intelligence. When I heard him decline the service by telling the proposer how he might be endangered, I formed my opinion of his being a man of no great courage, which after conduct proved to be the case.

and he even tried to *prevent* the Boston Tea Party.

The night before the tea was destroyed, I called upon Mr Hancock and pleaded against destroying the tea, and urged evil consequences that must follow upon it. 'Oh, he did not care; people might do as they would for him.' I then waited on Mr Samuel Adams. He was more artful; 'he could hinder nobody; but he would assure me it should not be destroyed that night...' – *and* I supposed had projected its being done the next.

But – most astonishing of all – Gordon also wrote directly to George III:

I dared to write to the first personage in Great Britain to mention my wish that the American Colonies might be gratified by the repeal of all the obnoxious acts relating to them – surmising that, was it done, in case of any future war with Spain, by the assistance of the Americans, all the Spanish Dominions in North America might be subdued and added to the British Dominions, and then the title might be – King of Great Britain, Ireland and North America. I enclosed the letter in one to Lord Dartmouth ... and my regards for King and Country *and* the American Liberties were therein manifested.

But, of course, Gordon's opinion was not the only one on this matter. A complete split between the American colonies and Britain was never desired by a lot of people – Washington himself, and John Adams, never really favoured it. But some believed equally firmly that it was necessary, and Tom Paine – another East Anglian voice on the American scene – trumpeted his own declaration of independence with passion (*Common Sense: Thoughts on the Present State of American Affairs, 1776*):

OLD MEETING HOUSE,
St NEOTS.

The sun never shined on a cause of greater worth. It is not the affair of a city, a county, a province, or a kingdom but of a continent – of at least one eighth part of the habitable globe. It is not the concern of a day, a year, or an age; posterity are involved in the contest, and will be more or less affected, even to the end of time, by the proceedings now. Now is the seed-time of continental union, faith and honour ... The cause of America is in a great measure the cause of all mankind. Many circumstances are not local, but universal, through which the principle of all lovers of mankind are affected ... The laying of a country desolate with fire and sword, declaring war against the natural rights of all mankind, is the concern of every man to whom nature hath given the power of feeling ...

And it was Tom Paine's opinion that won the day.

In 1786, American Independence achieved, Gordon came back to England – to a meeting house in St Neots in Huntingdonshire – and it was here that he wrote these letters to his daughter recalling his eventful travels in America. In 1788 he published a four-volume history of *The Rise and Progress and Establishment of the Independence of the United States of America*. Then, at last, when he was 82, he came back to the chapel at Tacket Street, where he had first heard the voice of Providence calling him to other things.

The Call of Providence? What if this man, now lying in this quiet spot in Ipswich, had had his way? What if the Boston Tea Party had never happened? What if George III had listened? Might not the relationships between Great Britain, Ireland, North America and other countries in a commonwealth of English-speaking nations have been very different? But Providence did not order events like that.

Even so, within the space of 25 years William Gordon had left Ipswich, been to America, been involved at the highest level in the War of Independence and, back in England, had written its history. The Call of Providence, whether assisted and directed by him or not, had certainly accomplished something. William Gordon, D.D., had been called to play a significant part in the making of that declaration which was to be so important – and remains so important* – in the modern world:

We hold these truths to be self-evident – that all men are created equal; that they are endowed by their creator with certain inalienable rights; that among these are life, liberty, and the pursuit of happiness. That, to secure these rights, governments are instituted among men, deriving their just powers from the consent of the governed; that whenever any form of government becomes destructive of these ends, it is the right of the people to abolish it, and to institute new government ... And for the support of this declaration, with a firm reliance on the protection of Divine Providence, we pledge to each other our lives, our fortunes, and our sacred honour.

* It seemed a strange coincidence that I came across the Rev. William Gordon and his story – in an English country churchyard – during the very year in which the United States of America was celebrating the bicentenary of its foundation.

6 By the Banks of the Wensum

> Now fades the glimmering landscape on the sight,
> And all the air a solemn stillness holds,
> Save where the beetle wheels his droning flight,
> And drowsy tinklings lull the distant folds...

The Reverend William Gordon may have felt called to a life of excitement, adventure and violent activity, placed as he was at the heart of events which were stirring and significant for the making of the New World, but the same was far from true of all clergymen and all parts of the world in his time. Providence called some men to much quieter ways of living, and in some parts of England the late eighteenth century was still a time of tranquillity. The world outside seemed filled with turmoil: after the American Revolution, the French Revolution flared into violence – aristocratic heads tumbled in Paris. The old order of Europe was shaking at its foundations.

But it still took ten long days for the news of the fall of the Bastille to reach villages in the English countryside and, even then, whilst noting this occurrence of 'a very great rebellion in France', a rural clergyman could be more concerned with 'buying an extra large crab from a travelling fisherman'. There were hardships in English country parishes, but there was also peace. And always – from then until now – far from the madding noise, busyness and complexities of the growing industrial world, the pastoral countryside of East Anglia has continued to hold something that can heal, something which really is like a 'psalm of green days' – 'making us to lie down in green pastures; leading us beside the still waters; restoring the soul...'

The still waters still flow by the banks of the Wensum, in Norfolk, as they have for centuries – easily and quietly. Green ways still lead away from them down to quiet country churchyards which are not only elegies but also excellent history books, filled with stories of ordinary people and ordinary communities, but with their extraordinary characters and surprises too.

Two hundred years ago, one of the most gentle and lovable Englishmen who ever lived, lived here – loving and enjoying these quiet waters. He was a country parson, but a parson with a difference. For one thing, he actually lived in his living and looked after his parishioners himself, instead of making do with an underpaid curate. But – did you ever hear of a rural clergyman buying gin and cognac from smugglers? merrily taking off a young widow's garter and good-naturedly exchanging a pair of his garters for a pair of hers? enjoying good food – a 'Pigg's Face and a pudding', a 'prodigious large pike – roasted – with a pudding in its belly' – and port and madeira to drink; and regular gambling (though for small stakes) at cards? This parson did all these things. The ways of God, which he nonetheless took very seriously, were always spiced with the ways of our mortality. And the church which he served well stands not far away from the banks of his much-loved river.

The man I mean is Parson Woodforde, of Weston Longeville near Norwich. A plaque set in the wall of the church was erected to his memory by his niece and nephew, Nancy and William, who came with him from Somerset to live with him: William for only a short time until, after several efforts, a place on board a ship was secured for him; Nancy

Weston Longeville church, as drawn by Parson Woodforde's nephew William, 1780

until her uncle died. But the chief reason why we remember Parson Woodforde, and why so many people now go to Weston to look on his plaque with affection, is that he kept a diary.

'ANNO DOMINI 1776...' this was the year when he first came to Weston, and every Anno Domini from then on was marked by a definite end and beginning. The year's affairs always drew to a close in December:

Dec. 3rd My frolic for my people to pay tithe to me was this day. Received for Tithe and Glebe £236. 2s. 0d. Dinner at 2. 17 dined – some dined in the parlour, and some in the kitchen. I gave them a good dinner: 2 legs of mutton boiled, salt fish, a fine sirloin of beef roasted, and plum puddings in plenty. They had to drink Wine, Punch, and Ale as much as they pleased. They drank of wine 6 bottles, of Rum 1 gallon and a half, and as for strong ale, I know not what – but suppose not less than 15 gallons altogether. Every person well pleased, and were very happy indeed. Some very disguised in liquour in the parlour! They all broke up about 10 at night. We had many droll songs from some of them.*

And every December 25th saw the celebration which Parson Woodforde instituted himself. He always had his rooms decorated with hulver (holly), and then:

Being Christmas Day, I lighted my great wax candle as usual, and the undermentioned poor old people dined at my house ... to each of them gave 1s. 0d. 7s. 0d in all.

Old Richard Bates	1s. 0d.
Old Richard Buck	,,
Old Thos Cushion	,,
Old Harry Andrews	,,
Old Thos Carr	,,
Old Robin Buck	,,
James Smith	,,

By God's blessing, I intend doing the same next Christmas Day. I had a fine sirloin of beef, rosted, and Plum Puddings. Gave old Richard Bates an old black coat and waistcoat.

Then they would all go off to church, and there Parson Woodforde would dispense one of his other regular Christmas charities:

To Weston Ringers: their annual gift of 2s. 6d.

On every New Year's Eve, too, as each Anno Domini began, Nancy and her uncle would make themselves snug by their own fireside, having

---

* *The Diary of a Country Parson: The Reverend James Woodforde 1758–1781*, edited by John Beresford, Oxford University Press, 1924–31 & 1968

filled their glasses in readiness, waiting for the clock's familiar chimes as the fire flickered warmly up the chimney.

We sat up tonight till after 1 o'clock on account of its being the last day in the Old Year. After the clock struck 12, we drank a Happy New Year to ourselves and friends in a glass of Gin Punch.

From then on, the year followed its customary course. Cold January days were spent in a regular 'rotation' of visits among good friends. There was Mr Du Quesne, a bachelor clergyman from Hockering; and Mrs Davy, the young widow whose garter Woodforde had once taken off; and Mr Smith, the studious vicar of Mattishall, who had also taken a fancy to her. There was Mr Howes, who was Woodforde's curate before he came to Weston, and Mrs Howes who soon unburdened herself to Woodforde that 'she lived very unhappy with her husband, as he wanted her to make her will and give everything to his family'. (Woodforde advised her not to do so!) And there was the charming, if not very robust, Betsy – Mrs Davy's daughter – a close friend of Nancy's.

They all spent the afternoon with us. I gave them for dinner a couple of rabbits smothered in onions, a Neck of Mutton boiled, and a Goose rosted, with a currant pudding and a plain one. They drank tea in the afternoon, played a pool of Quadrille after, drank a glass or two of punch, and went away about 8 o'clock.

But besides this 'Rotation Clubb' (which had its own rules – against the tipping of servants, for example), there were other good friends in plenty. Squire Custance, himself a very humane owner of a large estate, often drove over from Weston House, and Nancy was a great favourite of his wife, who tended to spoil her.

Mr. Custance, Snr., my Squire of Ringland, called on me this morn' – caught me out in the garden in a very great disabelle – in my Ermine old hat and wigg, long beard, and a dirty shirt on ... They behaved very friendly and civil to us ... Mrs. Custance gave Nancy a Pearl necklace, and pearl chain to hang from the necklace, a pair of Pearl ear-rings, and another pair of ear-rings. Mrs. Custance is exceedingly kind to my niece indeed.

The Squire's younger brother, Mr Press Custance, once caused a scandal in the community. It was not so much that he *kept* a mistress, Miss Sharman – that was a commonplace matter – as that he allowed her to sit in Parson Woodforde's own seat in church:

My squire called on me this morning and talked to me a good deal about his brother's mistress sitting in my seat yesterday, and whether she had leave, and also that she strutted by them in a very impudent manner coming out of church – and stared at Mrs. Custance! I sent to Mr. Press Custance's mistress to desire her not to make use of my Seat in the Chancel any more, as some reflections had been thrown on me for giving her leave ... Miss Sharman sent word back that she did not take it at all amiss from me – she knew from whence it came! – and she would get a new seat made.

But by and large, apart from notorious instances like this, the Squire and his family were well-liked in the parish.

In February, there was always Valentine's Day – but with a local custom very different from the one with which we associate it nowadays. Then, the children used to run round the village knocking on doors for pennies, and the benevolent Parson always gave more than his share:

Feb 14th To 36 children, being Valentines Day, and what is customary to go about in these parts this day – gave 3s od. – being one penny apiece to each of them.

During March, ponds might be cleared, and not only, it seemed, of weeds and mud:

My great pond full of large toads. I never saw such a quantity in my life – and so large! Was most of the morning in killing of them. I daresay I killed one hundred, which made no shew of being missed ... In the afternoon we took a large basketful of toads out of the pond, put them into a kettle, and poured some boiling water on them, which killed them instantaneously. Ben Legate, my man, took them up in his hands *alive*, and put them into the basket!

It may be a comment on the general sensitivity, in those days, to the pain experienced by animals that Parson Woodforde, a man so sensitive and benevolent, should speak so casually of killing toads in this way. When one of his dogs was incurably ill, too, he would kill it by hanging it. At the same time, however, the death of his favourite horse, Jack, could make him feel sick at heart and miserable for days. Dosing Jack with 'Gin and Beer' and attempting to bleed him had proved no use.

The death of my poor Horse made me very uneasy all the day long ... Am very sorry for him as he was so good natured a Beast ... Ben and Will skinned him. We kept one half of him and we gave the other half to Mr. Press Custance ... Fretting and vexing about my Horse made me feel much out of order today – quite low.

And he could also sympathize in good-humoured fashion with the accidental excesses of his pigs!

My 2 large Piggs, by drinking some Beer-grounds taking out of one of my Barrels today, got so amazingly drunk by it that they were not able to stand and appeared like dead things almost, and so remained all night from dinner time today. I never saw Piggs so drunk in my life. I slit their ears for them without feeling ... [And on the next day] My 2 Piggs are still unable to walk yet, but are better than they were yesterday. They tumble about the yard and can by no means stand at all steady yet ... In the afternoon my 2 Piggs were tolerably sober.

But times were hard not only for toads and dogs and horses. People, too, had to put squeamish feelings aside. There was the sad duty of burying the dead – a very frequent task in the days before inoculation for smallpox had been generally accepted. But also, a long way short of death, simpler ailments had to be endured:

Very bad all day in the toothache. The tooth is faulty ... My tooth pained me all night. Got up a little after 5 this morning, and sent for one Reeves* – a man who draws teeth in this parish, and about 7 he came and drew my tooth – but shockingly bad indeed! He broke away a great piece of my gum and broke one of the fangs of the tooth. It gave me exquisite pain all the day after, and my face was swelled prodigiously. Gave the man that drew it, however, 2s od. He is too old, I think, to draw teeth – can't see very well.

But as spring came on and gave way to the long days and light nights of summer, there were always – despite all the hardships – the great abiding pleasures of the countryside.

After breakfast, my man Legate and self rode down to the river upon a fishing scheme. We got two nets and had some men with us, and a cart to carry provisions for us as well as to bring home the fish for us. We were at it all day from Lenwade Bridge to Attlebridge. At one draught only we caught 59 brace of fish, mostly roach and dace, but some trout rather small. We caught, in the whole, about 6 score brace ... We all dined by the waterside upon some cold Beans and Bacon, and a cold rost leg of mutton which I had sent down. We left off about 8 o'clock in the evening at Attlebridge. For a pint of rum at Attlebridge for the fishers paid 2s od. Liquor had from Lenwade Bridge today – Ale: 30 pints; Rum: 1 bottle; Porter: 2 bottles. All of which I owe for there. We were all pretty tired by the time we got home.

Parson Woodforde loved a day's fishing, just as he loved, too, to go out with his three greyhounds, Duchess, Hector, and Reach'em:

Soon after breakfast went out a-coursing with my people and three greyhounds. Ran 3 hares and killed 2 of them – the hare that got off shewed the best sport. My young greyhound, Hector, performed incomparably. We also killed one rabbit. The first day of my going out a-coursing this season: very great sport!

And always, always, there were the sumptuous meals! Content and replete, being driven home with Nancy down the long, winding, tree-

* Reeves, who drew Woodforde's tooth, was also the man who had treated Jack, the horse.

sheltered drive from Weston House, Parson Woodforde's reflections were something like this:

We dined with Squire and Mrs. Custance, and Sir Edmund Bacon – who, I have to confess it, is more than a little cross-sighted – and Lady Bacon. And there was Mr. Smith and Mrs. Davy ... I do believe it must be true, as people are now saying, that there is an understanding between them ... Mrs. Davy! She seemed to me most impudent and saucy! Du Quesne was there – and Betsy – who is certainly become a fine young woman, though a little pale; and Mr. Paine and his wife – who has, you have to own, a prodigious long chin...
We had a *fine* dinner! A Calf's head, boiled Fowl and Tongue, a Saddle of Mutton rosted on the side table, and a fine Swan rosted with currant jelly sauce – for the first course. The second course: a couple of Wild Fowl called Dun Fowls, Larks, Blamange, Tarts, etc, etc, and a Good Dessert of Fruit amongst which was a damson cheese. I never eat a bit of Swan before, but – oh! – I think it good eating with sweet sauce.

Each Anno Domini followed its regular course, but there were times when unexpected troubles came, and some of them followed such a course and development that they can even be set out in the form of a story.

THE SMUGGLER: AND THE YOUNG MAN FROM LONDON

1. The Smuggler

One dark night it was so still that every slight sound could be heard. Indoors, Nancy and her uncle had abandoned their cards. They were tired. Uncle James was snoozing, when, suddenly, there was a low, barely distinguishable whistle under the window, then a thump. Nancy was startled. 'Uncle! Uncle!'

Parson Woodforde roused himself. 'Yes?' he murmured sleepily. 'Yes, my dear? What is it?'

'I am sure I heard something ... Listen! It was something outside I think.'

'Oh?' Her uncle was suddenly wide awake, and they listened. The whistle sounded again. 'Oh, ah, yes!' Woodforde was at once on his feet and making for the porch. 'It's Moonshine Buck,' he whispered back to Nancy, and then, as he softly opened the door, 'Come into the porch, Buck. What have we here, then? Something good I fancy?'

Moonshine Buck did not look like a smuggler. He was, in fact, the local blacksmith, but carried on his second trade with a certain degree of caution, and under cover of night.

'A tub of cognac, master, and one of Geneva, and a bag of tea – six pounds weight – if so be as you want it?'

'Indeed I do, Buck. Indeed, I do. And you must have a glass of something yourself! But, er – what, er?' He was always a little embarrassed over asking the price; but Moonshine Buck was not embarrassed.

'Three pounds for the cognac and gin – and three guineas for the tea.'

'Just a moment, my man.' Woodforde went off to rummage in a drawer, and then to pour out a good measure of rum. 'There is your glass, and there,' counting the coins into Buck's palm, 'is your money.'

'Your good health, master!'

'Good health to you, Buck, and ... silent as you go!' He took the swiftly emptied glass and lifted his finger to his lips.

Buck nodded, grinned, and was gone, and Woodforde motioned with glee to Nancy as he rolled the two tubs inside the door. Source of pleasure though it was (it was, in fact, quite a common transaction), nobody could have foreseen the worry that would follow.

2. A Sad Day – and the Young Man from London

The next day was a sad day, a parting of old friends, which Parson Woodforde recorded that night in his diary:

Our very good and worthy friends, Mr. and Mrs. Custance, with 5 of their children, with 2 nurses, and Rising the Butler, left Weston today – and gone to live at Bath. Pray God bless them and theirs, and may everything turn out to their most sanguine wishes. It made us quite low all day. It is a very great loss to us indeed.

And as sadness departed in one direction, what was to become trouble approached in another – along the road from Mattishall. Mr Du Quesne, Mrs Davy and Betsy had brought with them a quite unknown young man, all smart and fresh, it seemed, from London. There was an agitation and confusion of greetings – greeting each other and waving after the Custances' coach – as they arrived and got down. Woodforde was a bit unsettled and put out, just as Du Quesne was embarrassed at their having stumbled on a scene of leave-taking.

'Woodforde! Forgive us! I did not know the Squire would be leaving just at this time. Indeed, I did not know they were travelling today.'

'Du Quesne! What a surprise to see you. Yes . . .' They looked, together, after the vanishing coach, 'Yes, it is very sad. It will be a great, great loss to us. But, pray, where is Smith? Was he unable to come with you?'

'Ssssh.' Du Quesne hushed him, and led him aside. 'There is a sad story, I am afraid. I fear Smith has had a – er, well, a *miff* with Mrs

Davy. It seems he has broken it off with her, and she is hurt and upset about it and does not wish to talk. I beg you, do not enquire about him.'

Just then, the young man from London – a Mr George Walker, the nephew of Dr Thorne at Mattishall, who was also a friend of Mrs Davy and, indeed, doctor to them all – came near.

'But,' said Du Quesne, speaking up more loudly, 'Woodforde, allow me to present a guest of Mrs Davy's – Mr Walker, Mr Woodforde.'

The young man from London was very stiff, indeed with a distinct haughtiness of manner. 'How d'ye do,' he said.

Parson Woodforde was by now his usual, benevolent self. 'Welcome to Weston, Mr Walker. I hope we are to have your company in the neighbourhood for some long time?'

'Ah,' Mr Walker replied loftily, 'that must depend, Mr Woodforde, on matters of which I have, as yet, no knowledge. Mrs Davy has been so good as to invite me to stay. She informs me that the plays are good here at Norwich, and that there are other excellent entertainments. We shall have to see how Norwich society compares with that of London.'

Woodforde was wide-eyed, taken aback. 'Yes ... yes, indeed. Well, Mr Walker, I hope you will not expect too much of us, nor judge us

too quickly. There is not much hurry here in Norfolk, you will find – but I trust you may find things to your satisfaction.'

The young man from London bowed, but Nancy was now shepherding everybody inside. 'Do, I beg you, come inside all of you. We shall all talk more comfortably inside. I am quite sure you must be fatigued after your ride, and we shall have some tea in a moment. Please, please! Inside!'

3. The Message

As they were all trooping in through the door, Woodforde's man, Ben Legate, sidled up to him and caught at his elbow, trying to draw him aside – having been trying to attract his attention ever since the Mattishall party arrived. 'Master; begging your pardon – but could I have a word?'

There was always a touchiness about Parson Woodforde's relations with his servants. He dealt kindly with them and, by and large, they served him well. Certainly Ben Legate did, on an annual wage of £10. But perhaps it was just because of Woodforde's personal manner – the difficulty he always experienced in *not* being on good familiar terms with people, of whatever rank and station – that his men tended to take advantage of him, to get 'disguised in liquour' very frequently and, when so, to be more than a little disrespectful, so that Woodforde would decide there and then – at once, emphatically, irrevocably this time! – to terminate their employment ... only to relent later when tempers had cooled, and when mutual dependence and affection were again realized.

'Well, Ben?' said Woodforde, amused at his man's air of secrecy. 'What is it this time, then? What is all this about? Have we some sort of conspiracy here?'

His amusement quickly vanished, however, as Legate drew him further away from the others, and began to whisper. 'Well, master, I have just been told a message – on good authority – that John Norton, the smuggler, has been arrested, and that he will very likely inform on Moonshine Buck. And if so – why – Moonshine Buck might be pressed to inform on those who trade with *him*. I thought you should know, master. It could go hard, you might say,' he went on, with the suggestion of a smirk, 'if some folk was to be found with a tub or two in their house ... as evidence, you might say.'

Parson Woodforde was pale and shaken. 'My goodness, Ben! Yes ... yes ... Well, er – not another word, Ben. Not another word. And thank you, thank you.'

Ben nodded, and went round to the yard in something of a conspiratorial fashion – though with a smile on his face – whilst Woodforde, dazed, followed his visitors into the house.

4. A Surreptitious Burial

That night, long after the others had left again for Mattishall, and after he and Nancy had sat together for what seemed an interminable time, Woodforde began, uncomfortably – for it was so unusual – to pull on his old boots. Nancy, feeling low after the Custances' departure, but also a little excited by Mrs Davy's and Betsy's excitement over their new 'property', their guest from London, was herself feeling more than a little unsettled. She became increasingly irritated at her uncle's awkward, fumbling antics.

'Uncle, what *are* you doing? You are not *changing*, are you? Have you seen the clock? It is very late!'

'Nothing, dear, it is nothing,' Woodforde bumbled, 'nothing at all. I am feeling a bit low, and not a bit tired. I feel I must just walk outside for a while. It is not very dark, and I shall not be able to sleep, even if I retire.'

'Not dark?' said Nancy. 'Why, an hour ago I couldn't see a single tree on the lawn out there! But, well, I shall go upstairs. It has been a tiring day, and I have promised to visit Mrs Davy and Betsy tomorrow. You have no objection? They are to show Norwich to Mr Walker and would like me to go with them. Ben says he can take me on the mare in the morning, and I *may* stay the night at Mattishall because it is very likely we shall be late back from Norwich.'

At this, Woodforde, whose own touchiness was aggravated by his worry and sense of guilt – not at having received the liquor, but at the possibility of its being found in his possession – expostulated in a troubled, offended, aggrieved way. 'Norwich? Mattishall? Mrs Davy and Betsy? Why, Nancy, what can you be saying? Why have I not been told of this? And what is all this about Mr Walker? Mr Walker! Why, we have scarcely made this young man's acquaintance.'

'But Uncle, Mrs Davy asked me only during this afternoon; there has been no time to tell you of it.'

Parson Woodforde shook his head, as though unsure of himself. 'There is something *bold* about Mrs Davy. I do not know what has become of her, or of Betsy. I do not hold with these ladies any more. I cannot believe that my friend Smith would have had, er, a miff with Mrs Davy over nothing. It is not like him! It disturbs me, your going to stay with them … However, if you have said you will go, I daresay you must go. But I do not like it. I wish you to know that I do not like it!'

'Uncle, dear, believe me – there is no cause for you to worry. Ben wishes to start early, so I shall be no trouble at all. I will *try* to get back, but, at the latest, I shall be back the evening after tomorrow.'

Parson Woodforde subsided. Perhaps he was over-suspicious of Mrs Davy and Betsy, and the young man from London ... In any case, other things were pressing urgently on his mind! 'Well, perhaps I am being a little foolish ... unnecessary, perhaps – and, er, well, I just *must* go out for a while! Goodnight, then, Nancy. I leave it to you to do as you think best.'

'Goodnight, Uncle – and please do not feel there is any cause at all for you to worry.'

As Nancy made her way upstairs by the light of a candle, Woodforde went out of the porch, muttering. Nancy had been right. It was pitch dark, almost impossible to see, and he did not dare take out a lantern. He took a spade. There was a long period of thumps and grunts and shadowy movements under the trees by the hedge. Parson Woodforde was digging a hole in the garden and burying his two tubs of spirit. Nancy heard the muffled noises, came back to the stairs from her bedroom, and tried to peer out of the window. From outside, just a glimpse of her face could have been discerned in the candle-light. She, however, could see nothing, but knowing her uncle, she formed her own conclusions and smiled to herself as she went back to her room while the bumps and thuds continued.

5. *An Anxious Guardian*

The next night, Nancy did not come back. Parson Woodforde was alone in his study, and he was disturbed. Making his daily entry in his diary was giving him unusual difficulty. He lit a pipe, and wrote a little. He poured himself a drink, then wrote a little. Then he walked about, without writing anything at all. Then he sat down, and wrote again, from time to time picking up a note from his table and reading it again and again.

Feeling very low without my niece. Nancy behaved very pert to me yesterday evening. Being with Mrs Davy, she had learn't some of her extravagant notions. She talked very high all day. I talked with her against such foolish notions – which made her almost angry with me. I do not know what has become of Mrs Davy and Betsy: they have got so bold. And I most certainly do not like this Mr Walker. I do not like him. I do not like this Mr Walker's ways ...

And what is Smith thinking of? – sending me this note? – desiring me to meet him privately in Weston Churchyard? Have we all become conspirators, then? Have we all got beside ourselves? What can he possibly want with me there?

There was only one way to find out.

6. A Clandestine Meeting

If you had been there, in the small plain churchyard of Weston Longeville, two hundred years ago, you would have witnessed a strange scene. Among the trees, among the headstones, not far from the church door, the two clergymen met – both of them having had a fancy for Mrs Davy. They met; they stood; they walked about; and stood again, Parson Woodforde looking down at the ground as though deeply troubled and deep in thought, Mr Smith walking agitatedly beside and around him, gesturing, arguing, making his points emphatically, on occasion waving his hands in the air as though urgently desiring to prove an urgent case. It was a long meeting.

I stayed with Smith near an hour, talking over the affair between him and Mrs. Davy – by which he made out that Mrs. Davy was as artful and bad as any woman could be. It surprised me astonishing indeed. But . . . where is Nancy? What has come over my niece?

7. Mr Walker's Incivility

In fact, Nancy – who was very frequently bored in the heart of the Norfolk countryside, and said so, but who always behaved properly – did not stay away very long. The next day, Walker and Betsy drove her from Mattishall in a gig, but as soon as Parson Woodforde heard the sound of wheels on the gravel drive, he went out to remonstrate at once, almost beside himself with worry and annoyance.

'Miss Betsy – where is your mother? I wish you both to know that you have disobliged me very greatly in keeping Nancy away so long.'

'Uncle, *please*!' cried Nancy, angry and hardly able to contain herself. 'Do not speak to Betsy in such a manner.'

But Woodforde still addressed himself to Betsy, who was taken aback. 'I have had no way of knowing what might have become of her, and I think it has been very thoughtless of you all.'

'Uncle!' Nancy could hardly believe her ears, but her uncle then turned his tongue towards her.

'Pray be silent, Nancy! I shall want an account from you, too, as to why you have stayed away so long. This is hardly the way to repay the trust I have placed in you, I think?'

Nancy had alighted from the gig with Walker's help. He shook her hand, as though in sympathy and understanding as well as in parting, as she turned and marched past her uncle and into the house in fury. Parson Woodforde could not understand, and saw nothing in it but ill-mannered incivility:

Walker took his leave, and wished Nancy well by shaking her by the hand, and then went off with Betsy, and to me never said one word, or took the least notice of me. It was uncivil and hurt me very much indeed ... But what is happening to us all? What has become of my niece?

8. A Worsening Situation

Over long months, the relationship between Mrs Davy, Betsy and Mr Walker grew much closer. Indeed, it became notorious. Betsy and Mr Walker became engaged. And Nancy was drawn more and more into sharing their activities; more and more away from Weston Parsonage and her uncle. Often alone in his room, Parson Woodforde brooded over the pages of his diary, worrying, now, for his niece's own reputation.

Feeling very low without my niece ... What has become of her? I wish Nancy to break off every connection with Mrs. Davy and her long train of acquaintance. If she does not, she will disoblige me as much as she possibly can do. Nancy's character – being too intimate with Betsy Davy – is not talked of so well – as, more and more, she goes with Betsy Davy and Walker to Norwich by themselves. They all spent the day and slept at Mrs. Davy's when Mrs. Davy was away from home. Betsy's character is entirely ruined by her indiscreet ways – suffers herself to go for his wife at public places. Walker even boasts of his behaviour to Betsy and says the worst things of her ... He proves to be one of the most profligate, wicked, artful, ungrateful and deceiving wretches I ever heard of. I never liked him. I now believe both Mother Davy and Daughter also to be very cunning, close, and not without much art. I never wish to meet them again at my house, none of the three. But ... What has become of my niece? Nancy ... Oh, Nancy ...

But – for better or worse – situations, if we do not resolve them, resolve themselves.

9. Truth

There came a point beyond which the truth could be hidden no longer. The parson and others had long had their suspicions, but, suddenly, these were justified by facts that could not be denied. First one, then another, of Woodforde's friends received items of information, and hurried along to tell him about them. By the fire in the old Parsonage,

Mr Du Quesne and Mr Smith, excited and agitated, bombarded him with the news.

'You do not greatly surprise me, I must confess,' said Woodforde. 'But – oh! – I am astonished and surprised *how* bad it all is!'

'There is even a letter,' said Smith, 'from Walker's uncle to Barker the wine merchant at Norwich. He says his nephew is a profligate, abandoned young man – and to guard from trusting him with any money. He says he is allowing him £30 per annum to keep him from starving – providing he makes better use of it than he has hitherto done – but if he does not, he will withdraw even that!'

'What is more,' Du Quesne's normally placid voice was irate, 'he has used your *own* name – *your* name, would you believe it? – to get money raised for him at Norwich. He has had £300 of Mr Barker, besides more from many others. Why, he owes the King's Head – where he has dined with us often – as much as £50. He has even said that he is to marry Betsy Davy soon, that *you* are her guardian, and that he is to have her fortune of you directly on the marriage.'

'I cannot, *cannot*, believe it,' moaned Woodforde, getting up and walking up and down the room between his two friends.

Du Quesne was unable to contain his excitement. 'But even that is not all,' he cried. 'He cannot be found anywhere in Norwich. It is said he has gone off to Thetford – and was near £1,500 in debt. They say there are two writs out against him ...'

Parson Woodforde held up his hands, as though to say 'Enough!'

'I can scarce believe it,' he said, 'but, dear friends, forgive me! I must have Ben ride over to Mattishall and have Miss Nancy brought back home at once. There must be no argument! He must have her return at once ...' He walked over to the door, as though forgetting himself and already giving his instructions to Ben Legate; but then he turned back. 'But, what am I thinking of! – let me give you a quick glass before you go. I cannot tell you how much you have obliged me by bringing me this news, though, I must confess, it is little more than I had expected.'

10. Back to Normal

It was late in the evening when Ben and Nancy arrived, but Woodforde was impatiently waiting for them and opened the door and came out to meet them as soon as he heard their wheels on the drive.

'Nancy!'

'Oh, Uncle! Uncle, I am so sorry. Ben has told me all you have heard

– but I had just heard it, too . . .'

'Nancy! Thank God you are safe, and all is well.'

'I can scarce believe it is all true! I did not know these things at all – and I am sure Mrs Davy and Betsy did not. Poor Betsy is so distressed. I cannot say how sorry I am and I am ashamed at how foolish I have behaved.'

'Never mind, dear Nancy, never mind. It is all at an end. Nothing matters now. Come inside, come inside, and take off your cloak. Ben will bring your things . . .'

But as Parson Woodforde was about to lead Nancy through the door, he became aware that Ben was trying to catch his attention. 'Why, Ben. Yes, thank you, Ben! But . . . what is it? What is it?'

Legate had again assumed his conspiratorial manner. He drew Woodforde slightly away again from Nancy, and whispered. 'I have just been told a message, master – on good authority – that Norton the smuggler has been let off with only a small fine. He *did* inform on Moonshine Buck, but they could not prove much against Buck, and so *he* did not inform against anybody else at all, so . . .'

'Why, good fellow!' Woodforde was radiant. 'Good fellow! Nancy back home – and such good news!'

'I thought as you would like to know at once, master.'

'Indeed, and tomorrow, Ben, we shall have a large glass on it – a *large* glass! But just now, er, Nancy is just home, and I have to . . .'

'I understand, Mr Woodforde. Goodnight. Goodnight, Miss Nancy.'

'Goodnight, Ben – and thank you,' said Nancy from the doorway.

'Goodnight, dear Ben.'

Woodforde turned to Nancy, filled with a warm joy at seeing her back, and having the prospect of her more regular company and un-diverted affection again. But, at once, he began also to be a little pre-occupied as to how to get to his buried tubs.

'Now, Nancy, come inside . . . and you must be off to bed now. You must have a good rest tonight, and we can talk the whole day tomorrow. Everything can be as before – thank God! I must say, I am, er, a bit unsettled by all this. I think I must walk outside a little, before I go upstairs myself. It has, er, quite unsettled me, and there are still one or two small things I have to do.'

His eyes glanced away towards the hedge where the tubs were buried; but Nancy, too, could be understanding. She followed his abstracted gaze and smiled as they went inside. 'Yes, Uncle.'

That night was again one of thumps and thuds and knocks and

murmurings. But Parson Woodforde's confidence had recovered to the point of risking the dim light of a lantern. Soon, his tubs were dug up again. With even more glee than when he had first received them, he rolled them back into the house.

11. A Stark Ending

Troubles came – but troubles also came to an end. And one trouble ended starkly, tragically. The young Mr Walker, profligate, had also been the young Mr Walker, consumptive. Soon he was dead. Parson Woodforde received a fateful invitation. He recorded the event in his diary in very unemotional fashion; indeed, with a touch of hardness unusual in him:

Received a note from Dr. Thorne informing me of the death of Walker, and that he should be glad to have him buried at Weston on Thursday next...

Between 1 and 2 o'clock this afternoon, walked to Weston Church and buried Robert George Walker, aged 23 years. He was brought in a hearse with 4 horses, but from whence I know not ... I had a black silk Hat-band and a pair of Beaver Gloves. And the Dr. also gave me 1. 1. 0. There was not the least description on the coffin, or any kind of ornament: quite plain and uncoloured. At Quadrille this evening, won 0. 1. 0.

The young man from London had come and gone.

Parson Woodforde: a 'gentle and lovable' Englishman

12. New Beginnings

When troubles ended, there were even new, unexpected, joyful beginnings.

One June day, at five o'clock in the afternoon, there was a sound of wheels outside. Squire Custance and his wife and children had come back to Weston – and to stay! There were great rejoicings, and the meeting of good friends began again at Parson Woodforde's home. It was a great occasion, and one to be followed by many – when, for example, nephew William was able to come home for a time from his voyages, and when Samuel, Nancy's other brother, who was making a substantial reputation for himself as a painter, came to visit them.

Good times and the usual pattern of the year returned: the years went by; Tithe Frolics came and went; each Christmas Day the great wax candle was lighted. Old Richard Bates, Old Richard Buck, Old Thos Cushion, and other poor old men, had their Christmas dinner, and their shilling, and went to church to the sound of Christmas bells. And then there came that Anno Domini which Parson Woodforde could not record, when his own mortal span was ended. For some time, his 'feet and legs swelling' had made him feel uneasy. He had a low stool made 'to rest my legs upon, as they swell so'. Piles gave him some pain. He continued taking medicine, from Dr Thorne, 'but do not find, I confess, any great relief from the same'. And on New Year's Day 1803, the hand of the diarist stopped. The last words he had written – on Sunday, 17 October 1802 – were: 'Dinner today, Rost Beef, &c.'

Nephew Bill, on hearing of his uncle's death, set off at once from Somerset where he was staying, and travelled '238 miles without 1 minute's sleep' to get to the house of mourning. He and Nancy erected their memorial plaque in the church – never having the slightest notion of how many thousands of eyes would one day look upon it.

> 'His parishioners held him in the
> highest esteem and veneration and
> as a tribute to his memory
> followed him to the grave.
> The poor feel a severe loss as they were
> the constant objects
> of his bounty.'

But I am unwilling to end this story with melancholy or sadness. Parson Woodforde's diary is a living story of life as it was endured and enjoyed a long time ago, before the complexities of industrial society came down upon us all.

It is best to see him living still, enjoying the same green pastures that he loved – casting his nets by the banks of the Wensum, and catching so much of happiness – beside the still waters, which are still here.

7 The Voice that Breathed O'er ...
Little Stonham

> The breezy call of incense-breathing morn,
>   The swallow twitt'ring from the straw-built shed,
> The cock's shrill clarion, or the echoing horn,
>   No more shall rouse them from their lowly bed.
>
> For them no more the blazing hearth shall burn,
>   Or busy housewife ply her evening care;
> No children run to lisp their sire's return,
>   Or climb his knees the envied kiss to share.
>
> Oft did the harvest to their sickle yield,
>   Their furrow oft the stubborn glebe has broke:
> How jocund did they drive their team afield!
>   How bow'd the woods beneath their sturdy stroke!
>
> Let not ambition mock their useful toil,
>   Their homely joys, and destiny obscure;
> Nor grandeur hear with a disdainful smile
>   The short and simple annals of the poor.

The annals of the poor might have been short and simple; their destiny was no doubt obscure; but – sometimes at least – they contained plenty of life and colour. You will remember our earlier reliable East Anglian rule – that one clergyman leads to another! – and that one story in Mr Thurston's journal of newspaper cuttings which was pasted quite close to that of the Akenham Burial Case, carried the title 'Church Troubles at Little Stonham'. What troubles, I wondered, were these?

The gravestones in the quiet churchyard at Little Stonham (a tiny village just off the main road between Ipswich and Norwich) carry names like Tydeman – 'the parish clerk' – Edwards, Dorling, Frost. They lie peacefully enough now, but once these bones were stirred to a great passion. There was once a time when 'a voice that breathed o'er ... Little Stonham' came to be heard all over East Anglia.

Church and nation in England have always had their great clashes, but once Little Stonham had a revolution of its own. It was just a hundred years ago, and the people involved in it were so vivid as individual characters that, almost as soon as you start talking about them, you seem to see them walking through the village again: along the lanes, which have scarcely changed, or coming through the churchyard gates.

The trouble all began, it seems, with the coming of the new curate, the Reverend William Barlee. Mr Barlee was not a happy man. The youngest son of a rector of Worlingworth and a rich Jewish mother (his father had converted as well as married her), he had seen his three brothers make very successful careers in Law and the Diplomatic Service, one of them even becoming Governor of British Honduras and receiving a knighthood for it. His sisters, too, married well and became famous in their way – Louisa, the youngest, becoming the first woman missionary to the Jews and nicknamed (within the family) 'Ould Jerusalem'.*

William Barlee's lot was to have married Susan Victoria, granddaughter of James Gladstone, the brother of no less a man than the famous Prime Minister. Despite several letters from Susan and her mother to No 10 Downing Street, repeated over a number of years and begging for Church preferment, nothing was forthcoming. And so, William Barlee began his clerical life as a curate at Framlingham. What may have happened there remains hidden in mystery, but, in the high summer of 1870, one hot day in June, he came from there to Little Stonham, bringing his wife, Susan Victoria, and their one baby with him – none of them having any inkling whatever of what awaited them in this small village.

Mr Barlee settled in very quietly – some even thought ominously. He walked about, taking everything in, not saying much. He walked past the villagers; they walked past him. They acknowledged and spoke to each other, but not much was said. Still waters, they say, run deep, and people began to become suspicious. Rumours began to grow that he had left Framlingham because of some trouble with his parishioners. Certainly, it became clear that he was – well – truculent, and liked his own way. He seemed never to make up his own mind until somebody else made up theirs – and then he would decide the opposite. He was an awkward customer, and there were those among the villagers who formed the judgment from the beginning that he was much more

* For these family details, I am indebted to Miss D. M. Barlee, now of St. Felix School, Southwold.

interested in the church itself than in its members.

Feelings began to be established, to accumulate, to spread. Eyes began to flash, flicker and look down whenever he was seen approaching. Lips began to mutter. Gossip began to do its work. And all this mounting feeling began to gather about one fundamental issue. Should the services in church be read – or sung? If you had lived in Little Stonham in 1872, you could well have thought that the entire issue of the rights of man hung in the balance on this one question. The Reverend Barlee knew at least one thing for certain, and he took pains to make it plain to everybody. He, and he alone, had the authority to decide. But ... he was unable to make up his mind. And it is here that the other awkward character in the plot has to be introduced: Harvey.

Edgar Harvey was a rumbustious young labourer, known and liked by everybody in the village, full of life, full of himself and, in particular, full of an apparently inaccurate conception of the quality of his own voice which he felt obliged to spill into the ears of every bird, animal and man for miles around. It is hardly too much to say that Harvey believed he had been born to serve music and, in particular, to sing. When he came to the fields in the morning, he sang: the rooks scattered in a ragged squawking crowd out of the trees; the finches shot out of the hedges. As he worked away on his cart, he sang: and the horse stood by in a stunned condition, or jogged slowly and doggedly on in sheer resignation. In the firelit parlour of the pub at night, it was Harvey's voice, with those of his bosom-pals John Topple and Berry, that led the singing. Harvey loved everything musical, especially his own voice, and there is no doubt that he had a strong following in the village. How far the idea was official nobody ever seemed to know – indeed it was thought by some (including Mr Barlee) that an earlier churchwarden had sacked him from this 'post' – but it had certainly come to be taken for granted by many that Harvey was the choirmaster. When his voice rang out over the polished pews in the bare Little Stonham church, the congregation warmed to his enthusiasm. It was, at least, undeniable evidence of life – and of life warmly enjoyed. Everybody in the congregation, that is, except the Reverend William Barlee, Mrs Barlee and a new young lady who had begun to play the organ, Miss Smith.

Mrs Barlee found Harvey very vulgar. His voice might as well have been a foghorn as far as she was concerned. She wilted when it sounded. She and Miss Smith were the *musicians* in the church – those with a *knowledge* of music – and she and Miss Smith would decide about what music was played or sung, and the form of the singing. She gradually insisted on ousting Harvey and his choir from the singing gallery and having there instead, on occasion, a small company of children. Whether in rehearsal or in performance, Harvey and his voice now had no place at all. He had been edged out of things, and into a condition of smarting frustration. It was the same with Miss Smith. She, too, resented Harvey's presence in the organ-loft. Who was *he* to tell her about music? To choose the pieces? And besides that, he was too free, uncontrolled and clumsy altogether – a rough, rude, labouring type.

But if the Reverend Barlee was not certain about whether the services should be read or sung, Edgar Harvey *was*. Whatever a new, interfering upstart of a parson from Framlingham might think about it, he, Harvey, was going to *sing*. The voice that breathed o'er Little Stonham was not going to be stifled. The House of God was going to have music ringing among its rafters. One day in August 1872, in all the mounting bitterness of feeling, all the gossip of vacillating indecision, a juncture came.

The Reverend Barlee took his wife and family away for a long holiday – an event which none of his parishioners minded. The probability is that there were even smiles and waves when their gig sent up its farewell dust along the road of the village. While the cat was

Little Stonham church today

away, the mice decided to play. For six whole weeks, they sang their heads off – hymns and chants alike – glorious! All the time, the services were *sung*. All the time, the services were *enjoyed*. Harvey came into his own. His voice roared out in full liberty. The stained-glass windows shook and rattled with it. Warm eyes and hearts caught its enthusiasm.

When, six weeks later, on a Sunday, the Reverend Barlee drove back into the village, he heard what to others was a glad sound but to him was anathema. At once, this decided him. His mind was now made up; irrevocably. Harvey should not have his own way. From now on, services should *not* be sung – but *read*! In the week or two that followed, matters came to a head. Miss Smith and Mrs Barlee flatly refused to play the organ when Harvey came anywhere near. Barlee himself had more than one talk with Harvey to make things plain. And finally, Mrs Barlee even locked the organ, and sometimes the door to the organ-loft and singing gallery. From then on, whenever Harvey was anywhere in sight, only the harmonium could be used.

Music was silenced in Little Stonham. Ecclesiastical authority had clamped down. Nerves and relationships were tense, tight, at fever pitch. But ... some sort of plotting had been going on, and something, it seems, must have gone wrong with the lock of the door to the singing gallery. At any rate, on 6 October 1872, the crisis arrived. The afternoon service began – and took a strange course.

The congregation was large and attentive. Mr Barlee ended the reading of the first lesson quite normally. Quite normally, he asked his flock to stand and say the Magnificat; and, quite normally, he began to read it:

> 'My soul doth magnify the Lord
> And my spirit hath rejoiced in God my Saviour...'

But he had not gone very far when an awful and unbelievable sound jarred on his ears. How could it be possible? He stopped reading, his eyes rising in sheer disbelief and growing fury to the singing gallery which faced the pulpit. And there, standing at the very front, were Harvey, John Topple, Berry and two other young men – *singing* the Magnificat lustily and full-bloodedly. Their voices filled the church:

> 'For He has regarded the lowliness of his handmaiden...
> For behold, from henceforth all
> generations shall call me blessed...'

Mr Barlee flung out his arm towards them, as though issuing a command from on high.

'Stop! Silence! Silence I say.' But the male-voice chorus went on:

> 'For He that is mighty hath magnified me:
> And Holy is His name . . .'

Barlee thumped the pulpit and, seeing the local constable, P.C. Cook, in the pews below him, called out to him: 'Constable Cook! Remove those men from this church. Remove that man Edgar Harvey from that gallery.'

Constable Cook, however, looked undecided and ill at ease, and was, indeed, embarrassed and confused at having this sudden limelight thrust upon him. He looked sideways, indicating Mr Edwards who was sitting nearby, but Mrs Edwards put her hand out and restrained her husband from having anything to do with it, as the singers rounded off their performance in warm, enjoyable tones:

> 'And His mercy is on them that fear him,
> Throughout all generations . . .'

'Well, Reverend . . .' said P.C. Cook, 'I, er, I don't know. I think that's Mr Edwards' job, that is. That's the churchwarden who should . . .'

'P.C. Cook!' Barlee thundered – though, just then, Harvey, Topple and Berry were continuing with renewed gusto

> 'He hath shown strength with his arm . . .'

'I *command* you! Take those men out of this place of worship. Take them into custody. I . . .' Barlee kicked the pulpit door open with a loud bang and walked down the aisle. 'Come with me!' – and Mrs Barlee stretched an unavailing arm from her own pew in an effort to stop him.

'Restrain yourself, Willie. Don't get so excited.'

> 'He hath put down the mighty from their seat . . .'

sang Harvey and his cronies, looking down on the scene as Barlee stalked down the aisle to argue with P.C. Cook. And then the congregation began – in ones and twos, and then closely crowding on each others' heels – to stream out of the church.

'I tell you, Constable Cook,' cried Barlee, in passion, 'there is *no* churchwarden. I recognize no churchwarden here – not Mr Edwards or anyone else. I tell you, I *insist*, it is my responsibility alone. Now, please do as I *authorize* you. Be a good man – remove those men! This instant! They are breaking the law. I will not have my services wrecked in this manner.'

P.C. Cook turned miserably away, glancing up at the singers as he made his way to the door of the organ-loft, and they, in their turn, smiled down on him as their music continued:

'And hath exalted the humble and meek...'

They went on, uninterruptedly, as Cook came into the gallery and tried to remonstrate with them.

'He hath filled the hungry with good things:
And the rich he hath sent empty away...'

He persisted for a while, trying to argue with them, but then turned to look down at Mr Barlee, shrugging his shoulders and shaking his head helplessly.

'He remembering his mercy, hath
holpen his servant Israel:
as he promised to our forefathers,
Abraham, and his seed, forever.'

By this time, Barlee had been joined by his wife and Miss Smith – all of them standing immediately under the singing gallery and the five young men. Barlee was beside himself with rage.

'I will take him to court, I will! Such disgrace. Such behaviour. We shall see who is in authority here! I . . . I . . . Oh!'

He waved his fist, turned on his heel, and stormed out of the church; and then along the path and out of the churchyard gate, through the little knots of people who were standing about in agitated conversation.

Meanwhile, the Magnificat was sung to its resounding conclusion to an empty church:

'Glory be to the Father, and to the
Son; and to the Holy Ghost;
As it was in the beginning, is now,
and ever shall be.
World without end. Amen.'

Edgar Harvey, at the centre of his musical colleagues, closed his book with a satisfied smile.

That – or something very like that – is what happened on that October afternoon. Everything happened and developed so quickly, and was so confused, that it was difficult to tell with certainty *exactly* what happened and what was said. But soon there was an opportunity to reflect and think precisely about it, because Mr Barlee was every bit as good as his word. Three weeks later, the case was brought before Needham Market Police Court. Edgar Harvey was charged 'with having, on the

The singing gallery: scene of
Edgar Harvey's rebellion

6th October, maliciously and contemptuously entered a certain church
established by law, situate at Little Stonham, wherein a congregation
of protestants was assembled, and did disquiet and disturb the said
congregation by singing loudly during the service.'

There was a bench of four magistrates – two clergymen, one major
and one 'other'. One of the clergymen was Chairman – and he was as
nervous as a kitten, his hands and notes flapping about as wildly as his
words as he wondered anxiously about the various objections which were
put. Some of the villagers were there. P.C. Cook, John Topple and
others gave evidence to outline the story, as did Mr Barlee. But when
it was said that Barlee came from Framlingham, the solicitor acting
for Harvey – a Mr Watts – jumped in.

'What was the reason you left Framlingham?' he asked.

The Chairman flapped about at once. 'Stop, stop, stop!' he said. 'I am
sure that question is improper.'

But the clerk corrected him. 'That is cross-examination, sir.'

And Watts went on: 'Was it not because you made yourself so
disagreeable that the Bishop ordered you to leave Framlingham?'

'Positively not.'

'Was there not, shall we say, some unpleasantness?'

'No, there certainly was not.'

'Well, turning to October 6th, it surprises me that you ordered Cook, P.C., to remove Harvey from the gallery. Are you not aware that Mr *Edwards* has received instructions from your rector to act as churchwarden?'

'Mr Edwards has made no intimation of it to me. I repudiate him entirely. *I* am curate of Little Stonham, in *sole* charge, and I have been informed by the Bishop of Norwich that the appointment is in my hands.'

'I see, I see. Well, to come now to Harvey. Is there not some ill-feeling on your part towards this young man?'

'No. None at all.'

'Was not Harvey in the habit of leading the parish choir?'

'He was not.'

'Is he not, in fact, the choirmaster?'

'He most decidedly is not.'

'Well, was he not *considered* the choirmaster?'

'No sir. He is simply a troublesome fellow.'

'If your parishioners say to the contrary, would they be telling untruths?'

'Most decidedly they would.'

'Then your ministrations, I'm afraid, don't appear to have done much good (laughter). But it could be true, could it not, to say that the defendant has taken a very active *part* in the choir?'

'My answer is that he sang very *loudly*.'

'Ah – you have heard the defendant sing?'

'I have heard him sing.'

'Is it a very good voice?'

'*Not* a very good voice; not a very *musical* one.'

'Did he sing *particularly* loudly?'

'Above *all* the others.'

'You say that you have had complaints about all this. Who made these complaints?'

'Well, Mr Bloomfield, the *late* churchwarden, made complaints all the time. And, er, well, Miss Smith, the new young person who plays the organ, was continually making complaints. He was always, er, interfering with her. Always wanting his way with her.'

'That we all do, Mr Barlee ("Hear, hear," and laughter). Could you perceive him *start* the chant?'

'As quick as lightning, before I could get a word out.'

It seems a significant indication of the degree of support for Mr Barlee in the village that only Miss Ann Warren, the local schoolmistress, and Hannah Chittock, his servant, appeared as witnesses for him, and neither had very much to say. But then, before introducing his own witnesses, the solicitor acting for Harvey made this speech:

'Gentlemen, it has been the custom from time immemorial in Little Stonham, as in other churches – to chant those glorious chants to be found in the Church of England Prayer Book, and the parishioners feel so strongly they would have attended this court in a body to swear that there was no attempt on the part of the defendant – Harvey – to create a disturbance. I believe a few witnesses will be all that is needed to show that it was not the defendant who disturbed the congregation, but that there is ill-feeling and maliciousness against him on the part of Mr Barlee – and that it was from some selfish spleen on his part that the service of praise was disrupted; that he, Mr Barlee, has all along been the aggressor in this case...'

His first witness was then Mrs Edwards.

'Now, you are Mrs Laura Theresa Edwards, wife of Mr John Edwards, farmer, who *believes* himself to be churchwarden ... Will you say, in your own words, what happened in church that afternoon?'

'Well, after the first lesson was read, the Magnificat was chanted by some young men in the gallery.'

'Do you know these young men?'

'There were several there, but I saw Harvey amongst them.'

'Was it sung in an orderly manner?'

'Yes, sir, as I have always been accustomed to hear it sung.'

'Did you hear Harvey sing louder than the others?'

'Not at all. But it is usual for Harvey to take the lead in the singing.'

'When Mr Barlee called out to the singers to stop, did he call out in an improper manner?'

'He called out very *loud*! *Excitable*!'

'Did you hear what he said?'

'Yes, he said, "Turn those people out of the church."'

'Did Constable Cook do so?'

'No, he said he had no power inside the church.'

'You are quite at the mercy of Mr Barlee whether you have this service of praise or not?'

'Quite so.'

At this, Mr Barlee exploded in the court and had a sudden exchange with Mrs Edwards – ignoring the solicitor altogether.

'Have I not in my time paused in the service to allow you to get to your pew?'

'I don't think so. I never...'

'Isn't it true that people observed you to go out of the church that day with a triumphant smile upon your lips?'

Here the Reverend Chairman broke in again, flustered and excited, 'Stop a moment!' he cried. 'This is conjecture. Let us have something more tangible.' And he tried to bring the cross-examination back to a more even tone and temper. Mr Watts continued, still addressing himself to Mrs Edwards.

'Are you aware *why* Mr Barlee called out to them to stop?'

'Some time ago, he said there would be no singing if Harvey was in the gallery. He said that in the church out loud! He said, "Singing in the gallery can not be conducted to the Glory of God if *that person* is up in the gallery."'

With this, Mr Barlee put his head in his hands and moaned a little – though the whole court heard what he said: 'That is the only weak point I ever made in my life...' and that was the end of Mrs Edwards' evidence. The solicitor then called a Mrs Dorling.

'You are Mrs Elizabeth Dorling, and you are a regular attender at the church ... When Mr Barlee cried out, did you join in the singing?'

'Sir, I was too frightened.'

'Frightened? What frightened you?'

'Mr Barlee's manner. He shouted out to P.C. Cook, "I command you to take these men into custody!"'

'Is Harvey a sober man?'

'He is a perfectly sober man ... Mr Barlee has told me that he did not care *how* many came to church, he would as soon preach to the *walls* as to the people.'

This was said with a touch of spite, and again Mr Barlee exploded into the cross-examination: 'Did I not say rather that I would prefer a few *sincere* persons in a pew to a mass of people going to make a *spree* of it?'

'You said you only did your duty at church to have a comfortable home for your wife and family,' Mrs Dorling spat back at him with the same degree of viciousness, and again the Chairman waved his arms about:

'Stop, stop, stop! That has nothing to do with the present charge,' but the evidence went on.

All those whose names are now carved on the stones in Little Stonham churchyard stood forward to state their version of the facts. Thomas Frost said that Mr Barlee had 'busted' the door open, and seemed as if he would 'hull' everybody out of the church. He 'frightened every female in the church,' he said, 'and some of them nearly went into hysterics.' Harvey's fellow conspirator, John Topple, said that Mr Barlee 'spant' the pulpit door open. Denny the thatcher, Tydeman the parish clerk, and many others gave evidence. But, after all this, with the courtroom seething about them, the Bench decided (perhaps under the guidance of their timid Chairman) not to decide. Edgar Harvey was put on bail. The case, they felt, should go to a higher court – which meant, in Suffolk, Ipswich Quarter Sessions.

The tension of the whole affair built up over another three months. Then, early in January 1873, the case came up before a judge – Judge Henniker – and a jury. By this time, Little Stonham had become a hotbed of powerful feelings and, this time, the whole village *did* turn out. The public gallery was full, and it became pretty clear from their noisiness as soon as Harvey stood before them in the dock that the courtroom was not the *only* place in Ipswich where the Little Stonham contingent had been!

Feelings were running high, there were great expectations. All the evidence was the same, and therefore need not be repeated, except that Mrs Barlee added her own testimony. Counsel for Harvey addressed her in this way:

'Mrs Barlee, would you describe for us, as well as you can, Mr Harvey's voice?'

'Well, I would say it is, well, it is extremely distasteful and vulgar: a very uncultivated voice.'

Here there was beery laughter and some beery shouts from the public gallery, and hammerings and repeated cries of 'Silence in Court!'

'When your husband called out to the singers, is it true that you said, "Gently Willie"?'

'It most certainly is not.' (Titters and sniggers from the gallery).

'Was it perhaps, er, "Willie, dear, do be quiet."?'

'Indeed, it was not. I said nothing of the kind, nothing so absurd.' (Outright guffaws, continued and unruly, and again calls to order).

'Your husband was not excited or provoking?'

'My husband was never otherwise than perfectly calm.'

When the time came for the summing up, a fever-pitch of expectation had been built up, and each advocate made the most of his piece. First came the speech for the defence:

'Gentlemen of the jury, I will be brief. It is a sad spectacle when a clergyman comes into court to banter words of evidence with his parishioners, and resist their wishes. You have heard the evidence of almost the entire village, young and old, rich and poor, and I know you can judge whether you think Mr Barlee represents in his person that spirit of Christian charity without which no man should remain in a parish as a clergyman, be that parish large or small. I contend, and I believe you have heard enough to convince you, that it was Mr Barlee, by his own excited manner, who caused the disturbance. There is no doubt, alas, that a dreariness of services is being imposed upon the congregation in Little Stonham where there is nothing more tuneful than – Mr Barlee's tuneful voice. What is perfectly clear is that the village has said to a man – and almost to a woman – that they would rather hear Harvey sing a hymn *once* than Mr Barlee preach for a month!'

This brought loud laughter and the beginnings of gleeful applause, which was, however, quickly quelled as the opposing counsel rose to his feet:

'Gentlemen of the jury, I shall be even more brief. When some loud-mouthed ignorant labourer, who fancies he has a knowledge of music and a good voice, chooses to force himself on the congregation till the clergyman is compelled to take steps of this kind; and when an able counsel is employed to throw dirt at the clergyman so as to gain the applause of those in court who are filled with Ipswich beer, or something else to cause excitement ... the jury will understand the animus of the defence. There is nothing like roasting a parson for amusing the ignorant. Mr Barlee has had one desire only – and wants only to have the correctness of that desire upheld – to maintain his authority in his own parish church.'

Judge Henniker, too, was very brief and very clear:

'Gentlemen of the jury, we have heard a great deal on both sides of this case, but the point at issue is very simple. What you must have very clearly in your minds is this: Mr Barlee has the undoubted right to say whether the Magnificat should be said or sung. The only question is whether he had ordered that there should be no singing, and whether the defendant sang after being told not to do so ...'

There was then only the final question on which all the long months of disputation hung: 'Do you find the accused guilty or not guilty?' The judgment was definite, immediate, and greeted with uproarious applause: 'Not guilty, my Lord.'

And that – almost – was where the story ended. Not quite, however, because the Ipswich newspapers could not refrain from commenting on the case. It was obviously one more issue on which the side of 'dissent' (Mr Barlee's congregation 'full of Protestants') could attack the established order, and this called into the correspondence columns two interesting letters. The comment of the *Ipswich Chronicle* began like this:

HARMONY AT STONHAM

Was not the prosecution of the young man HARVEY for singing – albeit with an uncultivated voice, and in defiance of the Curate in charge – the Magnificat in Stonham Church, instead of saying it, an injudicious and undignified proceeding? Surely MR. BARLEE could have established his right as to 'saying' or 'singing' without resorting to magisterial proceedings. Did he try? There is something incongruous in a prosecution of this sort. One effect has been to empty the Church; another to make MR. BARLEE very uncomfortable; a third to return the uncultivated minstrel from the dock as a hero to the bosom of his admiring family; a fourth, to set pastor and flock by their ears; a fifth, to impeach MR. BARLEE'S system of management; a sixth . . . but there is no occasion to further enumerate points which are very obvious. When the case was heard by the Needham Market Bench we thought the wiser course would have been to dismiss it and to give a little friendly advice to both Curate and Singer. That Bench has, however, rather a relish for strict government – but, in this instance, it displayed scarcely its usual wisdom. The squabble about singing the Magnificat in Stonham Church was a trumpery affair, and ought to have been confined to the parish. In that event, the Court in Ipswich would have been deprived of some amusement, Counsel's attack upon MR. BARLEE would not have been made, and the parochials of Stonham would have had no opportunity of chuckling over the learned counsel's assertion that the congregation would prefer to hear HARVEY sing a hymn to hearing the Curate preach for a month...

It went on in the same vein, at great length, chiefly enjoying to the full its criticisms of Mr Barlee – and indulging in what Barlee's counsel had called 'roasting a parson'. The first letter it provoked, predictably, was one from Mr Barlee.

THE LITTLE STONHAM CASE

To the Editor of the Suffolk Chronicle.

Sir

I have no desire to criticise the article in your last issue headed "Harmony At Stonham", though I think it would have been in some respects differently worded had you been in possession of more of the facts of the case than you, sir, or the public, generally outside Little Stonham have been aware of. There are things which, on many grounds, it is inadvisable to bring forward in a court of justice, and, hearing the case as you did, I can understand a clergyman being thought injudicious who could find no other way of arranging the singing in his church than by summoning one of his parishioners before the magistrates. I have, however, all along been aware of the hidden hand at a distance that has been playing for a long time the game of which this has been a little episode. I entered the parish of Little Stonham under very peculiar circumstances, such as required great tact on my part, and for two years and more during the life of the late churchwarden, who supported me in everything, and who had turned off this young man, Edgar Harvey, from his employ for his conduct with regard to the singing, I kept things straight. Upon his death I had warning that troubles were looming in the horizon, but I had no idea they would take this shape! I am using a strong word, but one I am prepared to abide by, when I say the parish was demoralised at the time I came to it, and had I known half of what I have since learned, no inducement would have tempted me, or those belonging to me, to have come to it. I do not intend, however, now to resign this cure because a certain number of the people (by no means all of them) choose to leave the church, these being the very persons who did not leave it (for many did) when there was that going on in their knowledge (not unconnected with the singing) which, if anything, would have been a justification for their absenting themselves. No one of these people ever came to make a complaint to me or gave me any notice of their intention. With regard to the young man, Edgar Harvey, I have very little to say here. He has received all sorts of kindnesses from me. I had particularly encouraged him in his taste for singing, and he has certainly proved himself as provoking and impracticable as any young man in his position could well be to a clergyman. To your question in your article "Did I try other means?" I reply, every other means. Only when he became a tool in the hands of others, and broke the law (which everybody will allow he did), did I at last, having always declined before when urged to do so, decide to summon him, and, had I not done so, I should like anyone to tell me how I would maintain order in the parish or decency in the services. With one part of your article I cannot agree – namely, that the congregation should have a voice as to when the Magnificat should be said or sung. The only voice, in my view, to which they have a right, and of which the parishioners of Little Stonham never availed themselves, is that of coming to their clergyman and representing their wishes, in the confidence that if he feels able he will do his utmost to comply with them. It is entirely for those of them who have absented themselves, and who, one would suppose, are themselves the sufferers, to decide whether or no they will continue to do so; but, should they act otherwise, they will find their clergyman ready to take the very good advice, Sir, at the end of your article, to endeavour to "forget and forgive." I only say in conclusion of this already too long letter that while, in all likelihood, this communication, as is usually the case, may beget others, I trust I shall be able to keep to my present intention to trouble you no more. I feel sure I may trust to your good sense of fairness to insert this in your next issue.

I am, Sir, faithfully yours,
A. M. Barlee

Little Stonham Rectory, January 13th, 1873.

The second letter – perhaps less predictably – was from 'the uncultivated minstrel', Edgar Harvey himself.

LITTLE STONHAM AGAIN
To the Editor of the Suffolk Chronicle.

Sir

Will you kindly allow me to make a few remarks upon the letter in your last issue, headed "The Little Stonham Case". I do not wish to criticise Mr. Barlee, although I should like the public to know the errors of his letter – whether wilful or not I cannot tell – suffice it not to say it would have been far more becoming for a man in his position to have let the subject drop – for his own credit, not for mine; and I beg to state that the public outside of Stonham has been in the possession of more of the facts of the case that Mr. Barlee is aware of. They can quite understand how injudiciously he has acted in summoning one of his parishioners before a judge and jury at quarter-sessions.

Mr. Barlee says he entered the parish of Little Stonham under very peculiar circumstances, and that the parish was demoralised when he came to it. I will ask any sensible person if our present condition is not deplorable. We are as sheep having no shepherd – a scattered flock with no fold to shelter. Mr. Barlee says that Harvey has received all sorts of kindnesses from him. I should like to know whether it was in persuading the parishioners of the parish not to employ him or whether it was in trying to imprison him for singing the praises of God in his church. I can inform Mr. Barlee that his parishioners do not intend consulting him as to saying or singing the services; he can gratify his own taste, as he has done lately, by saying them to pretty well an empty church. Trusting that you will have the kindness to insert this in next edition,

I am, Sir, yours truly,
Edgar Harvey.

Little Stonham, Jan. 22nd, 1873.

That was the end of the matter, except for the outcome – although music and liberty seemed to have triumphed, they did so at the expense of an empty church. Who was mostly right and who mostly wrong, we shall never know. What we do know, however, is that within a few years Mr Barlee moved on to Intwood, near Norwich, and there is one part of his story that I have not mentioned so far. During his stay in Little Stonham, Mr Barlee had a second daughter, Mabel Susan. She lived for only 14 months, and lies at the north end of the churchyard under a small cross.

Mr Barlee had not been a happy man when he came to Little Stonham, with rumours, from Framlingham. Leaving Little Stonham with far more than rumours, he must have left much sorrow behind and taken a good deal with him. 'Character,' said Novalis, 'is fate.' Some men seem doomed to troubles.

But Harvey and his voice went on! He was only a young man at the time of the Little Stonham Case, but there are still some people in the village who remember him. They were children in the village school when he was an old man just before the First World War. And *how* do they remember him? Some simply as 'Old Edgar'; some as 'Spring-heeled Jack', because of his splay-footed gait – he was 'scrogg-footed' as they say in Suffolk. They remember him as a tramp-like figure, walking along the roadside wearing a tall hat; a labouring type who – as they put it (tapping their temples with the tips of their fingers) – 'had it up here'; often out of work, but always neatly dressed. And they remember him going from cottage door to cottage door in the village, alone, at Christmas time, singing carols, and – they are *all* agreed about this – with an awful voice! We know, too, that during the 1930s some Suffolk folk-songs were taken down here from a man who almost certainly knew Harvey.

The voice that breathed o'er ... Little Stonham, and brought something like fire and brimstone in its train, did, it seems, do something to keep music alive.

English country churchyards *are* elegies – green, sleepy, beautiful ... but evidently it wasn't always so. In God's little acres, our forefathers once saw stirring times!

8 Monument

The boast of heraldry, the pomp of pow'r
   And all that beauty, all that wealth e'er gave,
Awaits alike th' inevitable hour.
   The paths of glory lead but to the grave.

Nor you, ye proud, impute to these the fault,
   If memory o'er their tomb no trophies raise,
Where through the long-drawn aisle and fretted vault
   The pealing anthem swells the note of praise.

         *   *   *

Far from the madding crowd's ignoble strife,
   Their sober wishes never learn'd to stray;
Along the cool sequester'd vale of life
   They kept the noiseless tenour of their way.

Yet e'en these bones from insult to protect
   Some frail memorial still erected nigh,
With uncouth rhymes and shapeless sculpture deck'd,
   Implores the passing tribute of a sigh.

Near the centre of a large, rambling village, remote and little-known, just on the Suffolk side of the River Waveney – which has long divided the North Folk from the South Folk – isolated, beside a large rectangle of noble lime trees which whisper and rustle some 60 feet high whether a wind is blowing among their leaves or not, stands a large round tower. It broods like an ancient monument as it stares out of its great empty window-spaces over the surrounding fields. But, you wonder, a monument to what? There is no answer.

The tower is very old and completely empty. The roof, the floors, any internal timbers it once possessed are gone. It bears on its walls evidence of fireplaces. Someone once lived here. A few hundred yards away, round the foot of a slope of meadows, is a long-undisturbed moat, with only waterfowl among its dense reeds, and swifts and swallows dipping and gliding over it. Certainly, it was the site of the original manor house (perhaps a small castle?) of the village, and the tower once looked down on long ecclesiastical pilgrimages making their way from Bury St Edmunds to Norwich. They came in procession up the rough track in front of the tower to rest here. 'Barefoot Monks of various ranks and orders – a Bishop or a Cardinal preceded in procession by Lords, Ladies, Nobles and attendants – all walking barefoot to my ladies chapel, to St Christopher's Tomb at Norwich!' says the historian we shall soon come to. And he adds: 'Humbug the whole of it! – though they used to stop here to refresh themselves.' But the ghosts of all those who walked in such pageantry have long gone, and certainly the lime trees which now grow closely up to the tower, embracing and almost obscuring it, were not here then. So the mystery remains.

But as you come nearer to the tower, down any one of three ways from the inhabited parts of the village, you see that the tall lime trees

Wortham church as seen from the rectory fields

hide something else – a country churchyard. Seven centuries ago, in 1272, the parish church was built on to the tower. The tower itself – where it now supports only a small wooden bellchamber – was used as a church steeple. And the area bounded by the lime trees now holds only the frail memorials erected to the forgotten people of a country parish; and stones, of course, are limited and heartless things. They record, they seem durable, but they crumble and are overgrown, and time completely erases what is on them. In any case, they can never really recall *people*; what individuals were really like, what their characters and circumstances really were. And once there was a rector of this parish who thought the same. He wrote this about monuments:

We see monuments remaining in many parishes – but they tell only of the *Lords* of the soil, the deeds of ancestry, the virtues of the wealthy. How very few records have we of the *poor* people among whom we have lived – who toil for us while we sit at ease.

The poor pay for everything. Who makes the Queen's drapes silk or any of her Lords' and Ladies' clothing? Poor people! Who cultivate the lands? Poor people! Who obtain the luxuries of fish, flesh, fowl or anything else – but poor people? Who build the houses of the great, the palaces, or even the Temples of our land? Poor people! Who fight in our armies and navies? Who dig out the gold, or smelt it, or coin it? Poor people!

How many have lived among us with each his or her little history – and yet no record remains of their deeds. They pass away. Their graves are made in the dust – and not a single monument remains.

Richard Cobbold, who was Rector of Wortham for 52 years – from 1825 to 1877 – and who wrote those lines, was also given to poetry. He expressed the same feelings in this way:

> While all the great, the noble, and the grand
> Are now photographised throughout the land,
> How few are noted at our very door –
> Those whom we live with, as our Parish Poor.
> Yet, dear old friends, with whom I've spent my day,
> Though mostly gone – and gone God's happy way –
> When 'neath the village sod we all lie down
> And look to rise at voice of God's own son,
> May I with you receive the kingdom's bliss,
> In brighter, better, happier world than this.

And he decided to change all that – to create a monument with a difference to the poor people of his parish.

He could write (he had published novels like *Margaret Catchpole*) and he could draw and paint, so, throughout his life in the parish, he gradually created a monument to his friends which will outlive all the

Richard Cobbold, 1797–1877: *a simple record of days past among poor people*

Wortham Rectory, built by Richard Cobbold in 1827; his home for 50 years

stones in the churchyard: not something of stone, with only names and dates chiselled into it, but something warm with the many-sided lives of people, and with their feelings. First, he made a book of the people themselves, with a character-sketch on one page and a water-colour portrait on the other. Secondly, he made a similar book of all the places in which, in various ways, they lived in the village – the public buildings (church, school-house, workhouse), the mansions, farms, places of trades (smithies, windmills, shops) and the labourers' cottages. Many of these seem to be of pastel glazed over with – perhaps – white of egg. And then, at the age of 73, he re-wrote and re-painted all of these in only six months to make a 'splendid volume' showing the life of village people at their trades and in their homes.

Richard Cobbold's memorial to his friends was, in fact, no less than the first illustrated record of an English village community – a Victorian village – a monument which is unique. And though this sprang from his deep compassion for the poor and their destinies, something of the

Wortham Hall, home of John Johnson Tuck, a benevolent squire

conscious historian was there too. His monument, he said, was 'a simple record of days past among poor people. It may be singular to note the various costumes, or drapes, of our Parochial Poor at a certain period, and this will note it between the years 1869 looking backward to 1828'. He died in 1877 and, 100 years later, it is possible to go through the village with him and let him bring its past to life.

Cobbold's chief concern was to commemorate the poor but, to do this properly, he also gave a picture of the whole village: of the owners of the large estates, the tenant farmers, and their relationships with those who worked for them, and the poor. In general, he found good relationships between 'master and man'. Most employers in Wortham showed concern for their labourers during their working life, and found homes for them when their working days were done. Wortham Hall, for example, (later called the Manor House when the manorial rights were purchased) was the seat of the Betts family from the end of the fifteenth century until very recently. For almost half the period since the Norman Conquest this house has stood here, and the gravestone of the last member of the Betts family now peers out of a tangle of brambles close to the wall of Wortham church. But during one absence of the family the mansion was let to John Johnson Tuck, Esquire, and he certainly looked after his labourers.

Old Thomas Harbour [wrote Cobbold] was the best labourer for his years in Mr John Johnson Tuck's employ. He used to hold the Squire's Gray Horse at the Churchyard gate – and the horse itself is worthy of mention: I do not suppose the Squire ever had a better...

Mary Ann Harbour, his wife, prided herself on her 'technical education' in being an expert at breeding gostlings. 'Geese,' she would say, 'are more troublesome than ever I found my children. Aye, and they require more looking after, more humouring, more scolding, and sometimes also more thwacking than any obstinate child.' They know her well, and if she found one off her nest, when should ought to be on, it was quite ridiculous to see how 'Go you on to your nest!' would set the creature again as quickly as possible.

John Johnson Tuck, Esquire, obviously valued good servants also (such as Susan Fake, who had worked for him) and took a sympathetic interest in their personal problems.

Isaac Fake, who lived in Farrow's cottages in the Union Lane, always reminded me of the drawings I have seen of the poet Cowper. He was a good, patient, and pious man – and was carefully nursed by Susan, his daughter, who lived very much respected by John Johnson Tuck, Esquire. I made this sketch of him in his last illness because I admired the patience of the man who was supported through a long illness and never murmured once.

Another mansion was St John's, the home of the Harrisons, and here, too, a continual concern and charity was shown – by the Miss Harrisons especially.

Miss Elizabeth Harrison was indefatigable in her personal visits to the poor, and in her daily rounds distributed greatly to their wants ... She was beloved by all the neighbourhood and ready for every good work.

Miss Harrison also drew the poor people themselves into her efforts. It is obvious, for example, that clothing clubs – organizing a certain degree of self-help among the poor – were important then, as now.

Martha Buck, though in her 73rd year, is still able to help her, and trip over the fields and get over stiles with alacrity on her way to the Clothing Club under the auspices and management of Miss Harrison. What a way my aged poor will walk to pay their pennies into the Clothing Club that they may reap a present benefit.

Employers also took care of their labourers when their working life was over. A good example was Farmer William Read who lived at the Copper Beech Farm.

William Read always loved to be in the midst of the poor of the Parish of Wortham, for whom he always felt a kind regard and to whom he was always considerate ... A good farmer, a good employer, a kind hearted upright man.

Ted Collins and his wife Rose Collins who worked for him still live in a cottage near Mr. and Mrs. Read.

Ted Collins was the best labourer in the Parish – if honesty and integrity, steadiness and fidelity, activity and energy, be qualities to be admired. Up early, constant to his work – and understood all branches of farming from the hedgerows to the plough – and from pigs and poultry to sows and horses. Rose Collins was a very active farming woman – understood poultry, baking, and milking – a most capital dairy woman and in every respect an honest woman. What am I to say more for her? Why – only that I wish she were a little more constant at church than she is!

But Farmer Read was also very tolerant in allowing an idiosyncratic individual to sleep in his barn.

Old George Minter has not his equal anywhere in these parts. He is beyond all doubt the scamp of the county. He sleeps every night in Mr. Read's barn, has been sent to gaol 12 times for refusing to work and for vagabondism, and yet no reformation takes place in the man. He can scarcely be called sane and speaks in the pompous manner of the theatre. 'Yonder is my mansion, sir (pointing to the barn) and there let me tell you I sleep as soundly on my bed of straw as you do on your bed of down. I envy neither King nor Queen, Lord nor Lady, Priest nor Squire. I do no harm to anyone. I take what is given to me – and I would not thank anyone for more than my daily food! I am a philosopher – my

Isaac Fake, 'a good, patient, and pious man ... I made this sketch of him in his last illness because I admired the patience of the man who was supported through a long illness and never murmured once'

George Minter, 'beyond all doubt the scamp of the county ... speaks in the pompous manner of the theatre ... I have seen some of the profoundest men puzzled when they talked with him – and yet all his friends are ashamed of him' philosophy is this – *Be content!* I never was otherwise.' I have seen some of the profoundest men puzzled when they talked with him – and yet all his friends are ashamed of him – one gives him a herring, another a penny, another a crust of bread. If sent to the Treadmill he always comes out with a character for quietness – but the moment he is out – he is a solitary man again ... He sleeps with the cattle in the stack-yard, rolls himself up in the straw, and fears nothing.

Observing these kinds of relationships, Cobbold was content with many aspects of the established order of English rural life, and he said so quite plainly:

I heartily pray that the owners of the lands of Old England may flourish as well as the occupiers, and that the labourers may long reap down fields of plenty and be contented and happy.

> May all the Halls and Mansions of our great –
> As well as poor men's cottages – be made
> The residence of Christians' happy state:
> Who love their neighbours – and do not degrade.

Even so, he was not blind to some irregularities among the wealthy: that which had developed at the Grove, for example:

Mrs. Henry Balding at the Grove was made, sadly, a young widow. Then, one day, a young man – Mr. Barclay – rented the shooting, and took up his abode in the shooting season. Between him and the whole family a most romantic attachment has come to exist. The Wife of the late Mr. Henry Balding is most deeply attached to the said Mr. Barclay, and of course he is the same to her. He drives about with her – and journeys to London with her. All the work of the farm is carried on in the name of Mr. Henry Balding, but *he* is the manager and controller of the expenditure. There is a mysterious Romance in this which must one day come to light. But what will be the state when the secrets of all hearts shall be disclosed?

In much more serious ways, too, Cobbold was far from being uncritical of some aspects of village life in his day. He kept a close eye on the changing institutions of the Victorian village.

If you were to be asked which social institution lay most at the heart of the village in early Victorian times, what would you say? The Church? The great estate? Richard Cobbold would have been inclined to say: the Post Office. It was the Post Office which was beginning to change all village communities throughout the country, because, with the Penny Post and the New Poor Law, it was becoming responsible, in each locality, for administering the new policies of central government. It was the Post Office which most conspicuously heralded the end of distinct local communities in England and the beginning of a centralized state.

This is the Shop of Wortham. The Village Shop! Who in the Parish of Wortham can forget Mr. Charles Youngman Browne's shop? Here all the villagers go to post their letters, for the Post Office is here established! Here also the paupers of the parish go to receive the liberal dole of the Poor Laws, donations, grants, or merciful considerations of the Poor Rates. Here also the Relieving Officer meets them, and they receive their flour and their pence. Mr. Browne's shop is therefore a place to be much observed!

But Mr. Charles Youngman Browne also is a *man* to be observed! He is one of the craniologists, phrenologists, or free thinking men ... a very civil, well behaved, and well-to-do man – light hearted, lively and active, the most voluble talker, and ready for an argument at any time! Mr. Browne is a careful philosopher, I admit! – but ... I see no support of our school – though he is such an advocate of instruction; no attendance upon the Sacraments – though he is professedly a Churchman. He subscribes to the Clothing Club – but then – we lay out from 70 to 80 pounds per annum at his Shop for the very articles of clothing which we subscribe for. Faith must produce some good works – or it will not be seen to live!

Significant changes were also taking place in education. A weather-worn façade of the old school building still stands in Wortham, symbolizing Faith, Hope – and Charity lost in between! But Cobbold himself saw almost the whole history of education during the nineteenth century.

Rebecca Bobby – the Widow Bobby – was an old School Mistress who kept a Dames School. She was a very neat and tidy old Lady; mother of a large family; and kept this kind of preparatory village school for many years – and certainly carried by her quietness of demeanour much sway. She taught ABC, and how to thread a needle, and could and did teach cleanliness. But, alas, she knew little or nothing of the life eternal ... She was very ignorant herself, and, like many who teach young children, imposing rather than enlightening. But Dames Schools now are very much out of fashion. *Wonderful* infant schools and *wonderful* national schools!

Mrs Maria Jolly was a later village schoolmistress – known in her day far and near as the respectable old Lady who was cured by the far-famed digestible food called by the name of 'Revelanta' ... It is evident she thought something of her own scholastic powers because she required no puffing from others – being sufficiently puffed up within herself as to think herself wonderfully clever ... In one sense she *was* very clever, because any one may teach that they *do* understand but it requires a very clever person to teach that they do *not* understand! A very bad reader and a still worse writer – but very imposing, very grave, very commanding! Not a church-woman, but the centre of female preaching on the Ling.

George Howlett, the later Village Schoolmaster was also a specimen of a gone-by day – when the Fear of God was taught together with a competent degree of arithmetic, writing and reading – but the intricacies of science were not then taught with their ABC ... It was but yesterday that the examiner of the Union school complained to the Chairman of the Board and the Guardians concerning the ignorance of the boys in the school in these words: 'I find the boys very deficient indeed! They know nothing of Hydrawlics, Hydrostatics, nor Opticks!' 'Indeed,' says the Chairman, 'nor do I!' 'Nor I,' said another, 'Nor I, Nor I, Nor I,' etc, etc. 'Pray sir – will you be so good as to tell us what these things are?'

Sometimes, Cobbold was overwhelmed by the changes he had seen, and by the conditions of those who taught the children of the parish, and he himself was bound, to a large extent, to take responsibility for them.

What afflictions have I known in this old School House. I could positively drop my pen and weep when I think of them all . . .

The teachers have nothing to pay for rent, rates, or taxes. I pay them 10/– a week and they have the school pence. But this is as much as I can afford.

Chiefly concerned to help the poor, however, Cobbold was also especially concerned with the Union House, the Workhouse, and more especially still with the administration of the New Poor Law. It was here, and not among employers, Cobbold believed, that the worst evils and inhumanities of his day were to be found. It is a long-standing question whether the Boards of Guardians who administered the New Poor Law dealt with the poor in a humane fashion or not. Cobbold's experience left him in no doubt whatever: they did *not*. Nothing angered him more than the attitudes and actions of the new 'officers':

What a variety of changes have I known in this Union House since its first establishment in 1838. At its very commencement what a battle I had to fight. There were four old people – each exceeding four score years who could not earn a living. Old Will Paxman was one of them. That Christmas-time, an order was given *not* for the removal of these *paupers* into the house, but for their *'beds and bedding'* to be removed. In the depth of winter the Overseer and the Constable of the Parish by the command of the Guardian went and took these old people's bed and bedding from under them leaving without any order for themselves to go into the house, and destitute of any covering. Was not this an act of cruel oppression? I say it was. I suffered with those poor people. I got no justice for them – and many have been the anxieties and troubles in that house since. 'Man is born to trouble as the sparks fly upward.'

It was the same with Billy Rose.

Give Billy a shilling and he will live a week on it. He had not for 30 years made application to the Poor Law for relief and then he was offered three pounds to marry a wife in another parish! But one year he did so. The Chairman gave him an order for himself, his wife and children to go into the House – well knowing that he had no wife or child. They made a joke of him. Was it ever intended that the poor should be mocked by a public body? Oh England, thou art driving a mad career when, on this day as it is proposed in Parliament that the Unions should be made responsible for the finding of soldiers for the war, and yet be suffered to mock a poor man in his poverty!

But the most telling case Cobbold recorded was that of old James Harbour, a cattle dealer. James once lost all the cattle he possessed – 100 beasts. They were victims of Rinderpest, a scourge in those days. They started to drop to the ground when leaving Wortham Common, and were all dead before reaching the market at Bury St Edmunds. Harbour never got over this loss. It was a complete family disaster – his wife was driven out of her mind and had to be taken into Melton Asylum. It was a misery and humiliation to the old man to be forced, in his 79th year, to apply for poor relief. According to Cobbold, the case before the Board of Guardians was dealt with like this:

An attendant at the door let James in, and he stood in front of the Chairman who was busily looking through some papers. 'Master James Harbour ...' he said, still looking down at his papers. Old James nodded as his name was mentioned. 'Master Harbour ... Well, Master Harbour?' He looked up at him. 'You have a request to make, I think?'

'Well, Gentlemen,' James began uncomfortably, 'I, er, I can work no longer. I have a being* offered me by Miss Harrison's gardener, Hubbard, who lives in the Hill Cottage in the parish, but I cannot work at all. I pray you, Gentlemen – I can do no other – to grant me outdoor relief.'

'Oh, outdoor relief, eh? – that is what you want!' The Chairman noticed a neighbouring member of the Board beckoning to attract his attention. He leaned his head towards him, listened a little to his whispering, and then called out to James: 'Go out of the room!'

Startled, James turned and shuffled out with his rheumatic gait.

'Well?' The Chairman leaned back in his chair.

'This old man *can* work!' his colleague spat out. 'He was offered work on the roads – and he was too proud to go to it! Give him the *House*, I say, and let him pick oakum!'

The Chairman glanced round, 'Are we all agreed?' – and received nods from the others. 'Call him in,' he cried.

James was brought before them again, and the Chairman looked him up and down in silence for a while. Then, 'Master Harbour, cannot you work at all?'

'If I could, Gentlemen, I would not be troubling you. I am, er, afflicted with rheumatic pain which seizes me so suddenly that I drop all in a moment when I am standing in the wind ...'

---

* This seems to have meant 'a place to live', or 'a roof over one's head'. Some of the aged poor were given 'a being' in the back-sheds of their friends, and died there rather than go into the workhouse.

'Ah, well, Master Harbour – if that is your trouble ... Here is an order for the House for you! Perhaps you can do a little work in the workshop there without having to stand in the wind!'

Cobbold's own account of the case then ends like this:

> In silence deep – in grief profound –
>   The old man left the room
> And tottering beneath the wound
>   He reached his friends, he reached his home.
>
> He never more from bed arose,
>   He never more applied.
> He had relief from all his woes.
>   That very week, he died.

Of course, no one could be *blamed*! It was a *natural* death! No Relieving Officer could be blamed. No *Guardian*! No *overseer*! ... but there is a day of judgment to come!

He then marked a little Biblical reference in his text – I Samuel 2 v. 7 & 8, which turns out to be:

The Lord maketh poor, and maketh rich: he bringeth low, and lifteth up.
He raiseth up the poor out of the dust, and lifteth up the beggar from the dung-hill, to set them among princes, and to make them inherit the throne of glory: for the pillars of the earth are the Lord's, and he hath set the world upon them.

But Cobbold's chief efforts – and his 'monument' as a whole – were for the ordinary and poor people of the parish. Many of them lived on or near the Ling, an open place covered with furze, which they loved and where they used to cut turf (turf, not peat!) for the winter. It spreads out now, as it spread out then, from a signpost at the junction of several tracks, and from the doorstep of what is now a private house but which used to be The Tumble Down Dick. Here are just a few of the 'ordinary' people Cobbold knew, and, first of all, the proprietors of The Dick itself.

Ann Smith was cook, drawer of beer, hewer of sticks for the fires, and waiter on all customers from morning till night, and her difficult life with her husband ended in the workhouse. John Smith – her husband – was a hard working man – but a hard drinker as well ... He went mole-catching in the morning and drank with his customers in the evening. He and Sam Bartrum were drinking companions for years and years on Sabbath Days. Drink! Drink! Drink! His boast was that he had never been in a place of public worship and never would. When he lay dying, and wanted me to attend him, he said "Tell Sam Bartrum I implore him to attend his Church." But when I approached Bartrum, who was watering his horse opposite, he said, "Very good of him Master, but you haven't got a calf to dispose of, have you? That's more in my way."

Close to The Tumble Down Dick lived, and died, Richard Smith, known as Old Soldier Smith, a Waterloo Pensioner.

Soldier Smith served in the Peninsular Wars – he went out with the Duke of Wellington when he first took command of the campaign, and returned with him at the end of the war – and was an old Waterloo man. He could not do farming work, but used to work in his allotment and earn a penny by cutting turf for the winter. Old Richard was often seen to seat himself in his own-made wheelbarrow to rest himself. One day he sat down and never rose up again – but, as he sat, so he remained. A Pedlar's Dog, as his master passed over the Ling on his way to Diss, observed something in the old man which several who had passed him did not observe. That something was an unusual death. The dog went up to him, barked at him, smelt of him, and laid down at his feet. His master's whistle could not induce him to stir. The dog's conduct moved the attention of two labourers who were turning over a muckheap on the verge of the common. They came up to the old man – and then the dog immediately ran after its master. They found Richard Smith quite dead and seated as easy as if he were asleep.

Ann Smith, 'drawer of beer, hewer of sticks ... and waiter on all customers from morning till night, and her difficult life with her husband ended in the workhouse'

There was also another old Waterloo soldier in the village: John Bush, who had served in the First Grenadier Guards.

His description of the battle [wrote Cobbold] is like that of thousands of privates who know nothing thereof except the few minutes they have to fight. He had, on command, to lie upon the ground all the forenoon of the battle, and when the command was given him to rise and go with his regiment into battle, he was at first (he says) too stiff to go on. To him, the rest of it all appeared like a dismal dream. He had to sleep upon that dreadful field of carnage all that night amidst the groans and agonies of thousands of wounded and dying soldiers of various nations; and of all the enemies a dying or wounded soldier has to encounter, *he* says, none are worse than the camp followers, the plunderers alike of dead and dying and wounded.

John describes the scene as like a flight of vultures which he once saw, he says, after the Battle of Cadiz. To get knocked on the head and robbed after fighting for one's country may well be termed a sorrow. Surely if nations must have wars, and brave men must destroy one another, there should be a reserve to keep at bayonet's point the camp-followers at a distance – or there should be bands of mercy to minister to the wounded after the dreadful conflict.

But something more dramatic than anything that happened to him on the field of battle was nearly responsible for finishing John Bush off. Coming home one day after paying his rent on 'Mr Farrow's Rent Day', and having had a drink or two too many, he sat down to rest on the edge of the well in the garden. Putting his hand out to steady himself, he mistakenly clutched the chain which held the bucket, and disappeared head-over-heels backwards.

He went down sixty feet – into six feet of water – but survived. It was his own daughter who heard the rattle of the chain and so was the means of saving her father.

John's wife, Sarah Bush, was also a hard-working and well-known character in the village. She used frequently to walk to Burgate Wood – a distance of a mile or two – 'to buy a couple of faggots for fourpence of the woodman'.

In another of the poorer cottages on the Ling lived Old Moll King, a woman Cobbold much admired.

Old Moll King – Poor Old Moll – Dear Old Moll – was the active nurse of all the Parish. The poorest hovel – the tidiest and cleanliest people!
Moll King looks after poor Billy Rose – who is set off each morning with a few tracts which are given him to sell – not one of which he can read. He is fond of ringing the bells at Church – a quiet, well-disposed poor man – thankful for what is done for him, and contented. He shares Moll King's back shed with old Tom Goddard – and nothing will compel either of them to go into the work-house. Old Tom – a vivacious merry old man – said he never deserved a prison

– and never would go into one. Though he slept with Billy Rose in the outshed till the hour of his death – he always said: "I love the sight of the face of the open Ling on which I have cut turf from my boyhood and would rather give up the ghost there than be the tenant of the Union House in my old days".

George King: 'No man could talk more bigly, more scientifically, more knowingly . . . but in the presence of his strong-minded and strong-armed wife – and strong-tongued as well – he was always silent and overpowered'

But kind though she was to all the villagers, there was one person who did not benefit from this side of her nature: her husband! Old George King was the travelling barber of the parish – 'a very dapper and clean old man with aristocratic manners'. He was also a good talker.

No man could talk more bigly, more scientifically, more knowingly, to the gaping assemblies of the public house called the Dick, or at the Workhouse, or at the Mill, or at the various cottages at which he shaved. But in the presence of his strong-minded and strong-armed wife – and strong-tongued as well – he was always silent and over-powered. When a woman has an idea that somehow or another he takes more with others in personal administration than he ought to do, she is sure to take the shine out of him, by just letting them see the authority she has over her *lawful* Lord and Master.

'Now, George, what are you doing here at the Dick? You have no more customers here. I want you at home!'

A few minutes before, and George had been the life and soul of the company and appeared to be the most free and independent fellow in the world, but – "home, sweet home" – and to it George would go: strop his razors well, get in the turf from the Ling, feed the pig, listen to a lecture, and go to bed – but no more that day to the Tumble Down Dick!

There was Old Poll Parker, too, who dealt out at least one surprise in her time.

Old Poll Parker was the last in the Parish who used a spinning wheel – and had a spirit such as few women possess. In the time of the Volunteers, in the year 1797, she was attacked by 3 soldiers, who knowing her husband was on duty came into her cottage and assaulted her. She levelled them all three with a poker so that they had to be carried into Hospital and became the laughing stock of the regiment.

And there was also the usual village 'know-all' politician who, alas, was only ineffective.

Noah Fake, the Village Carpenter – the Village Politician – the Village Factotum – performing all offices – but knowing himself to be but a poor performer. Wishes to be right and yet does wrong. Will read all day – talk most deeply and seriously of his convictions – and in another moment set them all aside and give way to temptation! Anyone would pronounce him wise who knew him not.

An even stranger character than all of these was Judy Fuller who lived up on the Magpie Green with her perhaps over-benign husband.

Near the Magpie Inn – lived Judy Fuller. She always used to say to her daughters "Oh my dears, I shall not live another twelvemonth!" She was a living instance of giving way to inactivity before her proper time – like many who find it pleasant to their pride to be waited on. She took to her bed and kept it for 16 years. She always rejoiced to converse with persons of a superior education. James purchased the State Bed at the auction at the Hall – it was blue stuff and silver ornaments – a coat of arms hung worked at the head. But the cottage! Festoons of cobwebs hung like icicles from the black rafters. Nor would Judy permit the spiders to be killed. She literally enjoyed their society.

James waited upon her with all the tenderness of a good nurse. He was a pious, good old man.

But James Fuller was not the only patient man in the village. There was another well-known for his steadfastness of mind and his wisdom.

Here – on the Marsh – lived and died one of the quietest and steadiest labourers in the parish – a remarkable man – commonly called Wisdom Nunn on account not only of his being weather-wise, but from his quickness, and never making a foolish observation. He had very strong notions about us clergy – and would scarcely admit that we knew either the Way, or the Truth, or the Life ... God forbid that there should not be such to the end of time!

> Who wisdom keep in quiet way,
> Humble and cheerful in their day,
> When their day of work is done
> May rest in peace with Wisdom Nunn.

Judy Fuller, who 'took to her bed and kept it for 16 years. She always rejoiced to converse with persons of a superior education'

John Nunn, Cobbold wrote, was 'the first boy* in the village school to which his parents sent him (who thought him a prodigy) – but he had the wisdom to perceive and to say: "I know nothing." ' Obviously the Socrates of Wortham!

But Cobbold's sketches of individual people also contained accounts of incidents – some slight, some dramatic, some tragic, some comic – that he had experienced among them. Some were as light as a kiss!

In the New Cottage lived a dear child who loved me, and gave me the only proof of her love that she could give me – 'a *genuine kiss*'! ... I stood at my iron gate, holding it open for the children who were leaving the Sunday School. One little girl of the name of Woods, after going a little way on the road, returned, and to my astonishment, with tears in her eyes, put up her little face to kiss me. Next day, I told her mother, who said "She told me of it herself, sir. She said: Mother, as I am going tomorrow to London with Mr. Snelling's daughter, I thought I should never see Mr. Cobbold again – so I ran back and gave him a kiss."

Another account, too, told of Cobbold's love for children, and one old poplar tree still stands in Wortham where this incident took place.

The Poplar Farm is so called because of the lofty poplars which almost touch the house on the Long Green ... I shall never forget hearing one summer evening seven school girls singing 'Angels Ever Bright and Fair'. Though I had heard it many times in my life in the fashionable society of the day, I never heard it sung with half the happy expression of that day, and that at a farm house in the open air – at a holiday – at Poplar Farm.

Other sketches told of the country enjoyments which Cobbold himself loved and which he shared with his children – his three sons.

This is called New Waters because the lake which once existed in its front now nearly grown up with rushes was constructed after the old Lake behind the Hall. It used to be famous for its fish, and as the New Waters received all the tributary streams before reaching the old Lake, the fish were generally finer and fatter. This piece of water is fast growing up, and will soon – unless cleaned out – be a mere horse pond.

> Many the merry day gone bye
> When boys and I a-fishing went,
> When home from holidays, the fry
> Were on their fishing ventures bent.
> I grieve not for those days now past
> But hope – for others – they may last.

But others were more serious. Here is one telling example of how, in those days, the poor had to endure:

---

* i.e. the 'top boy' in the school.

Sam Dye became blind and deaf, 'yet did he never utter a single complaint'

Poor old Sam Dye was compelled to go into the gravel pits because of long afflictions following the loss of an eye. He was flushing a ditch for his master when he was startled by a hare leaping off the bank, and turning round to get a blow at her, a thorn pierced his eye which was wide open at the time. After a long, painful gathered wound, the eye burst, then shrank to nothing, and the eyelids closed up. He then worked in the gravel pits on the Ling, and his wife helped him. Then, one cold winter, Sam got inflammation in the other eye and became totally blind. To add to his afflictions, he also became very deaf – yet did he never utter a single complaint. I visited him when he was old, seated in his arm-chair, nose and knees together, near the fire, strapped by a girth round his body to the back of the chair to prevent his falling, as he once did with his forehead on the bars. In all these vicissitudes, he designed a two-wheel go-cart for Elizabeth which would drive lighter than a wheel-barrow, and she used to deal in herrings, coals, and a few cakes, and lollipops. Many a little boy and girl remember Mrs. Dye going to her long drawer for an half-penny-worth of sweets. Poor though they were, she would throw in an extra lollipop for no other reason than that she loved children.

And there were many stories of a problem which was widespread in rural, as well as urban life during the nineteenth century: drunkenness. Francis Groom, for example, was once the Parish Clerk, but had given way to 'sotting', as Cobbold called it. His story begins with the plaint of Francis Groom's wife. Cobbold writes here, incidentally, in the third person – of himself as 'the Rector'. Mrs Groom had said to him:

"I expect nothing less than that my husband will be found dead in a ditch, and be brought home to me a corpse..." but little did the Rector think that he should be the person to fulfil that prophecy ... Hear and read a fact very like it!

One day, the Rector was returning from the University Book Club which used then to be held at the old Scole Inn. In a watery lane leading from Palgrave to Wortham, the Rector's horse suddenly stopt, and directly across the road there lay old Francis. The Rector was alone in his gig. He put the old man in, and drove him to the cottage where he lived on The Marsh. The old woman's light was still burning. He found her reading. He broke the sad news to her – and she and her son George went to help to bring the dead man in. By some means, his head fell heavily on the gig-step – and there came forth an unearthly 'Halloo!' – which told them that the old man was only dead drunk!

Yet strange to say, from that day, the old man became a reformed character, for once and for ever terrified at the prospect of a drunkard's end.

Another story – though not about drunkenness – was even more dramatic.

Of the Widow Dye, a remarkable scandal was raised: that her husband who died at the Norwich and Norfolk hospital, and whom she brought home to be buried here, was not in the coffin. Some said she had sold her husband's body and that they heard stones rattle in the coffin. To such an extent did this report extend, that the poor woman requested me to have the grave opened, and the coffin also. I applied to the Archdeacon and the Chancellors of the Diocese, and had the proper

Francis Groom, 'terrified at the prospect of a drunkard's end'

authority for so doing – the Magistrates gave permission for the presence of the police, and the day was appointed for the exhumation. The clergymen, church-wardens and parishioners assembled in the churchyard. The chief accuser had to unscrew and take off the coffin lid ... and there in the sight of all men lay the remains of the deceased – poor man – in all the silent solemnity of the dead. Decently attired in proper grave clothes as he came out of the Norwich Hospital, an honour to the care and decency of that public institution and such a rebuke to the Slanderer that he never forgot to the day of his own death.

Truly did everyone afterwards respect the poor widow ...

What tales might be told of my village!

Some of the tales were as amusing as the Widow Dye's was tragic. Will Copping, for example, was a bricklayer, and used to take his grown-up sons to and from work in a cart pulled by a good cob pony. Cobbold tells how he 'came by' this pony. Cobbold's brother wanted to sell a 'good cob' and Will Copping wanted to buy one, so Cobbold himself acted as go-between. He sent Copping the horse, but not the price – which was £8 – and after a week's trial, Copping turned up. This was their conversation:

'I've come to settle with you for the pony.'
'How do you like him, Copping?'
'Very much.'
'I think he's a very valuable horse, Copping.'
'I think so, too, sir – and I arn't come to bid you a mucky price for him.'
'What will you give for it, Copping?'
'I'll give you nine pounds for him.'
'I won't take it, Copping.'
'Will you take twelve?'
'No, certainly not.'
'Well, I'll give you fifteen.'
'I won't take that.'
'Well, I'll give you one more bid. I'll give you twenty pounds for him. Will you take that?'
'No, I will not.'
'Then what will you take for him?'
'I'll take no such mucky price for him. If you take this horse, I will let you have him at my price, not yours.'
'Name it, sir.'
'Eight pounds.'
'Sir ... you're a Gentleman all over!'

'The money was paid,' wrote Cobbold, bringing the story to a close, 'and the pony went by the name of "The Old Mucky Price" till Copping died.'

Today, if you go through Wortham churchyard gate and take, say, 20 steps to the right, you come to the gravestone marking the place where Will Copping lies now. Take two strides to the left of this, and there is the grave of Richard Cobbold. The two friendly horse-dealers lying side by side in this country churchyard which Cobbold himself made into an elegy. It was he who, in the second year of his residence in Wortham, planted all the tall lime trees which now grow so closely about the ancient round tower of the village and shelter so nobly the resting-place of his friends.

Sometimes, events are very strange. Earlier, I mentioned the apparent coincidence of the discovery of William Gordon, D.D., and his letters, so near to the bicentenary of the foundation of the United States. Then there was the apparent accident of finding Joseph Thurston's newspaper-cutting story of the Akenham Burial Case just on the point of the centenary celebration of the founding of the *East Anglian Daily Times*, the paper which figured so prominently in this case. Something of the same kind is true here.

Richard Cobbold, who made this monument with a difference to his friends in his parish, died just over 100 years ago, in 1877. But then – his monument was lost. From that day to this, it has been hidden from sight – one volume in one place, one volume in another – on the shelves of second-hand bookshops or in county archives. Does it not seem strange that – just at the time when we are wanting to look back into the communities of the past which have made us what we are; just when we are thinking of the elegies of English country churchyards as history books – this record of the people, places and life of a village, which is a village history in itself, should have come to light? I said that in East Anglia there is one rule you can altogether rely on: that one clergyman always leads to another – and, curiously enough, many of them seem to have had a hand in this outcome.

Cobbold wrote one other small verse in his record.

> When time has past – should this poor scrawl remain –
>   Let some take pleasure who this book may gain:
> Pleasure to see how records may relate
>   The things of passing and of former date.

Well, his 'poor scrawl' – not so poor as the estimate his modesty gave it – *has* remained. Pleasure it has certainly given. But that is not all. Its message is the one towards which we have been feeling our way. In stories like these from English country churchyards, people who have been lost are found again. The hidden ancestry, the hidden heritage of our society can be better and more intimately known. Those who were actually at the roots of our communities are still there.

There are times when every writer has a strange experience – that something larger than himself is writing through him; that voices, characters, qualities other than his own, are working through his words; that all those who have ever meant anything in the making of himself (many of these quite beyond his own consciousness) are investing his words with dimensions of meaning and feeling beyond his own. He then knows that the truest estimation of his destiny is no more than to serve to the best of his ability all he has loved. In the writing of *this* book, in particular, I have had this experience to an over-powering degree. I feel, at any rate, a deep sense of privilege in being able to lift up, for the first time for all to see – in the same spirit, and (with television) in a way which Cobbold and his friends could never possibly have imagined – the 'monument with a difference' which he made so long ago.

Other words, too, spring to mind and seem fitting:

> Rejoice, ye dead, where'er your spirits dwell.
>   Rejoice that yet on earth your fame is bright,
> And that your names, remembered day and night,
>   Live on the lips of those who love you well.

I come back to the feelings with which we began. The places where the ashes of the dead are laid are the important centres of human community and human life. Here lie our true foundations on which to build.

Index

A HISTORY OF WESTERN MUSIC
Christopher Headington £1.95
A fully illustrated account of the development of song, opera, of
various musical instruments, musicians and music itself.

MANKIND AND MOTHER EARTH   Arnold J Toynbee £3.50
Arnold Toynbee's last book – a one-volume history of civilisation
that is breathtaking in its scope, scholarship and imagination.

THE PALADIN HISTORY OF ENGLAND
A new nine-volume history of England from pre-Roman to modern
times.

THE FORMATION OF ENGLAND   H P R Finberg   £1.25
Part of the new Paladin History of England series. This volume
deals with Britain in the Dark Ages between Roman and Norman
conquests.

THE CRISIS OF IMPERIALISM   Richard Shannon   £2.50
England in the realm of Victoria. A time of development,
expansion, colonisation, enormous social upheavals and reform.

PEACE, PRINT AND PROTESTANTISM   C S L Davies £1.25
Third in the Paladin History of England series. C S L Davies'
book deals with the period 1450–1558 encompassing the reign of
the Tudors and the breakaway from the Church of Rome.

ARCHAEOLOGY

THE CHANGING FACE OF BRITAIN   Edward Hyams   £1.75
How the geological structure of the land, our climate, our social
history and our industries have contributed to the shape of our
landscape.

THE DAWN OF EUROPEAN CIVILISATION
V Gordon Childe   £1.00
The last edition of the classic archaeological work that continues
to dominate all explanations of the growth of European prehistory.
Illustrated.

THE GOLD OF EL DORADO   Victor W Von Hagen   £2.50
The incredible saga of the quest for the Golden Man. The
world-renowned explorer and archaeologist reveals the culture that
inspired the legend and recounts one of the greatest real-life
adventure stories ever told. Illustrated.

INDUSTRIAL ARCHAEOLOGY   Arthur Raistrick   £2.25
The 'forgotten' aspect of archaeology; both an introduction and
an essential reference work from Britain's leading authority.
Illustrated.

MYSTERIOUS BRITAIN   Janet and Colin Bord   £1.95
All over the British countryside are totems and indications of
lost civilisations and knowledge, scattered in a rich profusion if
only the eye can see. This book looks into the past while suggesting
startling research for the future. Illustrated.

THE SECRET COUNTRY
Janet and Colin Bord   £1.95
More Mysterious Britain. An exploration of folklore, legends
and hauntings surrounding the standing stones, earthworks and
ancient carvings of Britain.

THE PILTDOWN MEN   Ronald Millar   £1.95
The case study of the most notorious hoax in the history of
archaeology. Illustrated.

HISTORY

AFRICA IN HISTORY   Basil Davidson   £1.95
A complete introduction to the history of the 'Dark Continent'.
Illustrated.

ART AND THE INDUSTRIAL REVOLUTION
Francis D Klingender   £1.50
One of the most original and arresting accounts of the impact
of the new industry and technology upon the landscape of England
and the English mind. 'There is no book like it.' *John Betjeman.*
Illustrated.

THE BORGIAS   Michael Mallett   90p
The rise and fall of one of the most notorious families in
European history: legends of poisoning, incest, and political
contrivance. Illustrated.

THE CHRISTIANS   Bamber Gascoigne   £2.50
Nothing has traced such an intriguing pattern through the past
2,000 years and involved so many cultures as the story of the
Christians. Based on Granada TV's internationally acclaimed
TV series. Illustrated.

THE COMMON STREAM   Rowland Parker   £1.25
The history of a Cambridgeshire village from the first traces of
human settlement to the present day, and the common stream of
ordinary men and women who have lived and died there.
'Beautifully written imaginative and truthful.' *Ronald Blythe*

ENGLAND IN THE AGE OF HOGARTH
Derek Jarrett   £1.50
An absorbing history which effectively debunks the traditionally
cosy view of the eighteenth century as an age of elegance and
freedom.

THE ENGLISH MEDIEVAL TOWN   Colin Platt   £2.25
The definitive study of the life, work, architecture and people of
medieval England. Illustrated.

EUROPE'S INNER DEMONS   Norman Cohn   £1.75
The history of the vilification of minority groups as scapegoats,
by the author of THE PURSUIT OF THE MILLENNIUM.

EVOLUTION OF THE HOUSE   Stephen Gardiner   £1.50
A history of dwelling places and domestic architecture from the
cave onwards. Fully illustrated.

FOLK SONG IN ENGLAND   A L Lloyd   £1.50
The classic history of the natural expressions of the British people.

FOOD IN HISTORY   Reay Tannahill   £1.95
Man's real history in his search for food; the measure of civilisation
is man's attitude towards food. A vastly entertaining and
authoritative panorama. Illustrated.

*All these books are available at your local bookshop or newsagent, or can
be ordered direct from the publisher. Just tick the titles you want and fill
in the form below.*

Name ....

Address ....

....

Write to Paladin Cash Sales, PO Box 11, Falmouth, Cornwall
TR10 9EN.
Please enclose remittance to the value of the cover price plus:
UK: 25p for the first book plus 10p per copy for each additional book
ordered to a maximum charge of £1.05.
BFPO and EIRE: 25p for the first book plus 10p per copy for the next
8 books, thereafter 5p per book.
OVERSEAS: 40p for the first book and 12p for each additional book.
*Granada Publishing reserve the right to show new retail prices on covers,
which may differ from those previously advertised in the text or elsewhere.*